# BLOOD

# IN OUR BOOTS

*Ed Haider*

EDWARD P. HAIDER

Scripture taken from the HOLY BIBLE, NEW INTERNATIONAL VERSION. Copyright © 1973, 1978, 1984 International Bible Society. Used by permission of Zondervan Bible Publishers.

**National Library of Canada Cataloguing in Publication**

Haider, Edward P., 1921-
    Blood in our boots / Edward P. Haider.

ISBN 1-55369-807-X

    1. Haider, Edward P., 1921- 2. World War, 1939-1945--Personal narratives, American. 3. World War, 1939-1945--Prisoners and prisons, German. 4. Prisoners of war--United States--Biography.
I. Title.

D811.H315 2002    940.54'7243'094381    C2002-903612-7

# TRAFFORD

**This book was published *on-demand* in cooperation with Trafford Publishing.** On-demand publishing is a unique process and service of making a book available for retail sale to the public taking advantage of on-demand manufacturing and Internet marketing.**On-demand publishing** includes promotions, retail sales, manufacturing, order fulfilment, accounting and collecting royalties on behalf of the author.

Suite 6E, 2333 Government St., Victoria, B.C. V8T 4P4, CANADA
| | | | |
|---|---|---|---|
| Phone | 250-383-6864 | Toll-free | 1-888-232-4444 (Canada & US) |
| Fax | 250-383-6804 | E-mail | sales@trafford.com |
| Website | www.trafford.com | | |

TRAFFORD PUBLISHING IS A DIVISION OF TRAFFORD HOLDINGS LTD.
Trafford Catalogue #02-0620    www.trafford.com/robots/02-0620.html

10    9    8    7    6    5    4

# Acknowledgements

There are some men with whom I served who are mentioned in the pages of this book. Out of respect and to protect the reputations of these fine men who dedicated their lives to the protection of our freedom and way of life, I have taken the liberty of changing some of the names.

Some of the men I served with in the Stalag Kommando deserve special mention. There was Andy Haralak who became a very good friend. Andy was a father figure to those of us who were incarcerated with him. There were my good friends Jim Henessey and Al Albert who escaped from Schulenberg one day when we were all out working the fields. God bless them–I sure hope they made it and had a wonderful life. LaMar Hardy was another close friend who I remember fondly.

I want to thank Mary Haider for her hours of editing this book; and, Bonnie Berger for providing the title after reading through the manuscript with me.

Frank Matas, a very talented, art teacher at Lake Park High School in Roselle, Illinois, receives my warm thanks for the wonderful cover illustration and several other sketches. A number of young, aspiring artists have my heart-felt appreciation for illustrating the book, including several of Mr. Matas' students: Constance Ciway, Deyana Matt, Jacob Messinger, Jennifer Wiecek and Scott Wold, who contributed sketches to make the text come alive within each reader's imagination. I want to express my gratitude to, Jim's and Mary's niece, Jessica Stacy, who also provided a number of sketches.

Finally, I want to thank my son, Jim, who has been my typist, editor and business manager throughout this project.

# Preface

Writing these memoirs would not have been possible without the help of my sons, Jim and Tom. Never having been much of a typist, Jim transcribed all my handwritten notes and assisted in the editing. Both of my boys were instrumental in my writing down my war experiences. If not for just knowing what I contributed to the nation's war effort, for my grandchildren and their children to someday say, "This is from my grandfather, it is his story of his time in the United States Army, 82nd Airborne Division, during World War II. Grandpa lived in the hands of the German people while he was incarcerated during the war."

These words honor all those men with whom I served. It honors the memory of the friends with whom I suffered at the hands of the Nazis. Should any of my friends or former war buddies read these words, or any of their family members, I hope they will contact me so that we can reminisce and see how we have faired throughout the years.

At the conclusion of the war we were thoroughly debriefed as to our experiences in combat and in the prison camp. The officials wanted to know how we had been treated and what sort of experiences we had witnessed. We were admonished then to tell no one what we had revealed to them. It has been a long time.

Over fifty-seven years have passed since those dark days of global turmoil and our nation is now on friendly terms with our former adversaries. Many official histories have been researched, written and published concerning the war and the experiences of the participants. This is my story and it is time that my family and others know what really happened.

# THE BOOTS FIT

"We're gonna hafta slap,
the dirty little Jap.
And Uncle Sam's just the guy
who can do it."

Back in June 1942 the world was in turmoil. The war was the topic of conversation everywhere. *Japan was moving at will throughout the Pacific, facing little or no resistance; and Germany was tightening its strangle-hold on Europe and North Africa.* Some of the boys from the neighborhood were starting to be called up for the draft. The little ditty that I mention above was only one of the many songs that were constantly being played on the radio, getting all of us fired up to serve our country and get involved in the fray.

Several of us, Spike, Tommy, George, Harold and I were overcome by patriotism and went downtown St. Paul to sign up. First we went down Rice Street to an enlistment office. There we ran into Mr. Hoffman. He asked us what we wanted and we told him we were there to sign up. Well, he must have thought we were just fooling around, because he told to us to get out.

Not to be deterred, we went downtown to the draft board at St. Peter Street and Sixth. We walked into the enlistment office and there sat a big ol' sergeant who, to us greenhorns could have been a general for all we knew. The sergeant politely asked if he could help us to which we answered, "Where do we sign up for the service?"

The sergeant said, "This is the place. What branch of the service would you like to join?" Not knowing any better and wanting to show my bravado, I said, "How about the parachute troops?" I figured this was something new and not many fellas went into that. I figured I would give it a try.

He said, "Sign here and take this paper home and have your father sign it. Bring it back tomorrow." I took the papers home and told my dad that if he signs me up, I would only be gone for about a year and then be out. Dad figured I wouldn't rest until I could get into the service with the rest of those who were signing up and leaving. As for my patriotic friends who went with me to the enlistment office–I was the only one to return the next day. When I told the enlistment sergeant that I wanted to become a paratrooper he said, "By all means."

Two days after turning in my papers I was on my way over to Fort Snelling, just south of the Twin Cities. My friends Harold and George and I made our first trip to Fort Snelling where we were all given physical examinations. We all were hoping we were in good enough health to pass. I prayed I would pass the physical and do just fine. Well, we passed all right. We were mustered into another building, asked our sizes, and issued a set of uniforms. The stories everyone had heard about military uniforms were discovered to be true. The cap fit just fine; the shirt was a little loose; and the pants were fair. But the boots! The boots were something else. We were in the army now! At least until they told us we could go home that night and report back at 0800 the next morning. Kenny, a friend of mine from South St. Paul, gave me a lift home on his motorcycle.

When I got home in my new uniform, my dad took one look at me and asked if the boots came with paddles--they were a little large. Next morning Kenny picked me up and we were off again to the world of the army. Kenny and I were so impressed with the food at Fort Snelling that we didn't think being in the service was so bad. Military life was pretty good –they permitted us to go home the first few nights–until we shipped out for Camp Wheeler.

# SUMMER IN GEORGIA

Military life to this point had been several days of paperwork. Finally, we were marched onto a troop train, right there in Fort Snelling and headed south for Camp Wheeler, just outside of Macon, Georgia. For three days we read, played cards, slept and just looked out the window trying to imagine life at Fort Snelling. We expected Georgia to be warm, but when we arrived in Camp Wheeler it was downright hot. We were wet from sweat all the time and couldn't wait for a shower. Camp Wheeler was just a temporary camp–used during the war for training. There were so many barracks–and they all looked alike. We figured we would never find our way back to our own if we ever left. This is where the army turned us, and several thousand others, into soldiers–six weeks of basic infantry training.

Learning weapons was a big part of our training. We were familiarized with the M1 rifle, the old 1903 Springfield rifle, Thompson submachine gun "Tommy gun", .45 calibre pistol and of course, the proper use of the bayonet. The practice dummies were hung for us to learn on and before long the straw-stuffing was shredded. We used the 30 calibre water-cooled machine guns as well as the air-cooled ones. Mortar training was also included. We fired the 60 and 81 mm mortars--these were wonderful weapons. They didn't take much to transport and you could fire them from anywhere. Camp Wheeler was all marching and learning weapons, and then marching some more. We endured some long marches with full field packs. These packs were basically used for bedding, but carried some other essentials too: blanket, mess kit, shaving kit, and the extra pair of dry socks.

One day while lying prone on the rifle range, a lieutenant by the name of Leopold came up behind me and ordered me to switch the rifle to my other shoulder. I explained to the lieutenant that I was left-handed and had shot

3

a rifle left-handed all my life with no problem. Just then, the deep voice of one of the captains, Captain Adair, who had been observing the practice from a nearby tower boomed over the field, "Lieutenant, leave that man alone, he is doing fine." This did nothing to endear me to Lieutenant Leopold, but at least I continued to shoot left-handed.

The obstacle course was certainly the Army's chance to get us acclimated to what lay ahead. We crawled on our bellies beneath the foot-high barbed wire while the instructors fired .30 calibre water-cooled machine guns over our backsides. Tear gas exposure was also part of the training–holding one's breath and learning the proper use of the gas mask.

The Georgia summer was warm and sticky. On the long marches we would all be soaked from head to toe. We always carried our field packs along with our gas masks which were suspended over our shoulders in their canvas cases. The gas masks were put to good use–most of us used them for carrying our stash of candy bars.

The marches provided us some interesting scenery in Georgia. We passed long tobacco sheds where the leaves were hung for drying. Some people had cattle, cows, horses, pigs and nice gardens. And, of course, there were the peanut fields. But mostly there were tobacco plants. The march was hot and dusty along the roads. Every hour the Army in their mercy gave us a ten minute break. We'd sit down and have a smoke. We soon learned that if you scratched the sand you could come up with a handful of peanuts. We tried them but they weren't too good.

Captain Adair, our company commander, surprised me one day as we all stood at attention during our morning review. He was walking up the line looking us all over when he stopped and approached me. Right out of the blue he asked me if I was left-handed. I told him I was and inquired how he could tell. He said I had my belt in the opposite way from all the others. I was amazed that he was so observant.

Six short weeks at Wheeler and our company of about 200 men were on our way in August of 1942 to other assignments. Some to infantry, some to artillery or wherever the Army had need. Ten or twelve of us, including two buddies from Minnesota, Kurt and Ed, were on our way to Fort Benning, Georgia.

Fort Benning has a long and illustrious history. Named after Henry Lewis Benning, a Georgia congressman, soldier and Justice of the Georgia Supreme Court. During the Civil War he served as a major general under Robert E. Lee, earning the nickname "Old Rock." Fort Benning opened as an Army Infantry school in October 1918.[1]

Fort Benning is a permanent Army Fort and the home of the 82nd and 101st Airborne. Benning was much larger than Wheeler, more men in training and more land. Benning came with an airfield for the C47's, C53's and C54's, with the primary plane of the paratroopers being the C47. At Fort Benning we were going to be turned into the Army's future parachutists.

At Benning the training intensified: no more walking, we were double-timing it everywhere. There was half a day in self-defense training and packing parachutes. This seemed to take a lot of time, as it should, you didn't want to make a mistake. We had judo lessons for self-defense in the saw dust pits. When you were in the saw dust pits you did not want to make the mistake of spitting. If you got some sawdust in your mouth, you just ate it. Spitting would get you a hundred laps around the field; and, for every non-commissioned officer you came across, you would stop, and tell him, "I must not spit in

---

1        Home of the Infantry–A Proud Heritage, Website of Fort
         Benning, www.benning.army.mil.
         (192.153.150.25/fbhome/heritage.htm.)

the sawdust pit." Of course you didn't always have to run laps, sometimes you were told to do 75 push-ups. When you finished they would ask you how many you did. You would tell them 75 and they would tell you to do ten more for *not* cheating. Many times during this training period I asked myself, "What in the world am I doing in this outfit?" Then I would think about it and realize not everyone can do what we were doing, so I would strive to do that much better. The training was rough and lasted from daylight to dusk–forever moving at double-time speeds.

One of the side-benefits of parachute training was the food–simply the best. Our meals included steak and other meats, potatoes, veggies, milk, coffee and dessert–three times a day, and all you could eat. They told us they would feed us good because they were going to work us hard.

Every morning, bright and early, after breakfast we would line up and stand at rigid attention waiting for the camp whistle to blow. As it blew, the instructors would come running out of their barracks and we would whisper to each other, "Here, come the gorillas." They did look like a bunch of apes–wearing T shirts with a big parachute on the front. We all stood there at attention until the gorillas were finished looking us over.

The training sheds were nearby where we would do the 40 foot rope climb. If, however, after reaching the top you decided to slide down the rope, the instructors would have you climbing back up again. After several weeks of grueling training we advanced to the 300 foot tower. Fort Benning had two of these towers that looked like they went all the way to heaven. Three hundred feet is just a football field standing on end. These towers were made of steel and had four large arms stretching out from the sides of the towers. The arms were controlled by the ground crew with a sergeant in charge. The control cables were electric and could be stopped anytime they so desired.

With one of the tower's arms you were lifted in what

we called the "buddy seat." The buddy seat got its name because two fellas would go up together. You would ride up in a canvas swing seat–all the way to the top. When you reached the top it would unhook and you came down under control. Most of the 'buddies' who went up were both on their first trip up the tower–not me. I happened to be the lucky one selected to go up the buddy seat with one of the lieutenants.

I thought, "He is so busy that we will go up and come right back down." But, I was wrong. He told the sergeant to stop the mechanism right on top, just before it unhooked. We got in the seat and up we went. When we got up to the top he started a conversation! He talked about what a beautiful view it was. "Look at that! You can see for fifty miles from up here." he said. Well, I couldn't see anything because I was keeping my eyes closed. When he asked me how I liked it, I told him I thought I was going to be sick. Then the Lieutenant discovered that we could get the seat swinging. Now I really thought I was going to be very ill.

After we completed the buddy seat jump we went on to the other arms of the tower. Each arm on the tower was somewhat different and used to expose us to different positions. The second arm lifted you from the ground in a prone position with a harness strapped to your back. The third arm of the tower lifted each of us by the shoulders. The last arm took you up in a parachute harness with the chute already open. At the top of the tower the chute was released and you floated down in the open chute. This gave us the experience of dropping in an open chute prior to actually jumping from a plane.

Everyone carried a small piece of paper with them to the top, kind of like a golfer who throws some grass in the air. At the very top the sergeant would call up to you with a bull-horn and tell you, "Drop your paper," to determine which way the wind was blowing. You descended accordingly, trying to avoid being blown into the tower. Using the chute's risers (canvas webbing straps that were part of the harness) we could turn the chute to steer away from the tower if the wind was blowing the wrong way. On occasion someone would be blown into the tower, but this didn't happen too often. They were very careful about our being blown into the towers since this could seriously injure someone.

There were a number of fellows who refused to cooperate. These guys were brought down and told to remove their boots and report back to the barracks. These folks were not considered worthy of wearing the paratrooper boots. These fellas would have to walk back to the barracks in their socks. They were the Washouts. They didn't continue in the program but were transferred out into other infantry units. Not everyone is cut out for or suited to be in the paratroops. It was constant, rigorous training–it's understandable that not everyone could take all that was dished out.

Along with everything else we were learning, like dismantling our weapons blindfolded and putting them back together, we learned how to pack a parachute. Everyone had to learn to pack their own chute. Each chute had a card denoting who last packed the chute and who last jumped with the chute. Each time it is packed or jumped, the card is signed by that person and dated. The chutes were only kept for 100 jumps and then discarded.

Prior to actually jumping from a plane, we jumped out of a mock-up plane and came down to the ground on a cable. The mock-up plane was only about twenty feet high. We would jump out this fuselage while attached to a cable to simulate the experience of jumping out of the plane. We would then ride this cable to the ground. This exercise taught us to tumble up when hitting the ground to break the shock of landing.

We were all anxious and excited to go up and make that first big jump. The first jump was at about 1,200 feet, followed by four more at only about 400 feet, just slightly higher than our training tower. Twelve hundred feet was fine for training purposes, but in combat we had to jump at 400 feet or less–any higher and you would be a nice, big target hanging in the air and the enemy could pick you off like ducks in a shooting gallery.

For that first jump we were all nervous and praying-- not knowing what to expect. When the red light above the plane's door went on, the jump-master says, "Stand up, hook up." All twenty-two of us stood up and at the jump-master's command we checked each other's equipment. Upon the command to stand in the door, we all shuffled forward. The pilot lifts the plane's tail and begins a descent, the light above the door turns green and the jump begins. The jump-master taps the first guy on the back of the leg and yells, "Go!" We then all file out, as close as we can get to one another. Sometimes you even got a face-full of silk. When you jump, your right leg goes out first, gets caught by the wind and turns your whole body toward the rear of the plane. Frequently you will see your chute go right over your head as it is blown by the propeller.

The nicest feeling of course after leaving the plane is when you get the opening shock of the chute–then you know it is open. An old-time sergeant told me to put on the chute's harness so tight that it was uncomfortable. This would keep the straps from tearing your shoulder skin upon opening. The shock was so bad that a lot of guys would have their leather boot laces just burst when their chute opened. We all knew we had to make the required five jumps to earn our wings–a small metal badge with a parachute in the middle.

Oftentimes someone would refuse to jump. Various reasons and excuses were given for not bailing out the door of the plane, so the chutes were taken and examined for whatever cause or excuse had been given. If someone else packed it and signed the card, that person would jump it to prove the chute was safe. However, if the chute was not packed properly, everyone would soon know. This happened a number of times. The fellow who packed and signed the card was taken up and had to jump. If all went well, the guy that refused was washed out of the outfit. During all the training jumps there was a jump-master in the plane to supervise the jumpers. His job was to make sure everyone was hooked up to the cable in the plane, and for good reason, if the chute is not hooked it won't open during the jump. There were times when a soldier would be so nervous that he would stand up, hook up his chute, then suddenly unhook and sit back down. Then when everyone is going out the door, he gets so excited, runs up, and out the door he goes! When this happened the jump master would go out the door after him. The jump-master would try to catch the falling jumper's static line, but this just is not going to happen since both jumper and jump-master are falling at the same rate of speed. Nonetheless, an attempt was made to save the soldier's life.

Very rarely did this happen, but I do know of a couple of guys who went out the door and didn't hook up first. The jump-master feels like he is responsible and he goes out the door and tries to save the soldier's life. There have also been cases where a soldier would just be sitting there and slide out the door. When this happens you just hope you don't get a late opening or get the chute caught on the tail of the plane. Generally this results in the parachute getting wound up over the tail of the plane with the jumper flailing and thrashing about in thin air. In one instance the jump-master scaled the static line and released the chute from the plane's tail, culminating in his own free fall. Both of these guys ended up okay on the ground, but this was one awful experience for both of them. It took a lot of courage on the jump-master's part to attempt to free the chute.

The army is no respecter of weather–we also jumped in strong winds. Strong winds prove to be disastrous. I broke both legs and most of the other jumpers were injured too. Some broke arms, some legs and one even broke his back. My third jump was the one that got me–broke both of my legs.

The wind that day was blowing at 27 mph and all the planes were contacted to come down, except ours of course. At that time we were over panel, the area of our drop, and we jumped. As I came down there was a jeep in the exact spot I was headed for. I yelled at the driver to move the jeep and he did just as I hit a few feet from it. A medic came over and asked if I was alright and I told him I was–until I tried to get up–I couldn't. He was waving a red flag to signal for an ambulance and away I went.

Our reward for this painful experience was timeout in the base hospital. This place was a real zoo. At meal time it was a race between crutches and wheelchairs; crashes were common with men, crutches and chairs flying in every direction. Stamina kept us going and we would pick ourselves up and continue on. I spent a number of weeks in the hospital. The whirl-pool treatments were great so I found myself in the whirl-pool everyday. I thought it was the best healer. The whirlpool was a huge tank, almost like a cow's watering tank. We sat on high stools and the water was as rushing and as hot as you could possibly stand it.

One of my partners in therapy was a young lieutenant who had made a night-time jump. We were all taught that when you are about to land in water, to release the chest and leg straps and when you are about twenty feet over the surface to jump out of the chute. Well, water shines at night from above–unfortunately, so does a black-top road. Needless to say, the lieutenant released and hit the highway. He injured both his hips and legs. I didn't find out about his injury until we got to know one another. No one wants to share their mistakes, and he felt pretty foolish about how he got hurt. We spent a lot of time together in the whirl-pool and visited each day–but to this day I can't recall the lieutenant's name. He was from one of our neighboring units and I don't believe I ever asked him where he hailed from.

Furloughs and time off were next to impossible to get. Only way to get time off was to have an accident or break an arm or leg. Even when you got some type of furlough, the army couldn't wait to get you back–making your furlough as short as they could. Just after my legs healed from their breaks, I got seven days off. Of those seven days, it took me two days to get home and of course I knew it would take two to get back. I made the most of my three days in St. Paul. It wasn't much time, but I was very happy to get that. Time off was really special–when someone would break a leg on a jump you would see them crying from pain and shouting with happiness and glee, "I'm going home! I'm going home!" That's how tough it was to get a furlough.

Following my recuperation of about six weeks, I was summoned to the Base Colonel's office. The Colonel wanted to know if I wanted to stay in the paratroopers or get out and transfer to an infantry unit. I wasn't going to let a couple of broken legs, which had now healed, keep me from being a paratrooper. I told the Colonel that I would love to stay if he could get me back with my buddies. He assured me that this would be no problem. But, first he pulled out a small foot stool from behind his desk. He told me to get up on it. Then he said jump down off of it and I did. He told me that I would do just fine. I found out that the army has a heart of sorts. I was back on my feet and going to rejoin my unit. Boy was I ever proud when the Commander pinned the paratrooper wings on my chest. We all felt just a little more special than the regular rank and file infantry soldier. And our pay increased too!

# WINTERING IN NORTH CAROLINA

In October I caught up with my group at Fort Bragg in North Carolina. We were assigned to the 504th Infantry Company of the 82nd Airborne Division. We lived next to the 101st and developed a lot of friendships with them. Bragg was no picnic. The training was extensive. We were back to double-timing it everywhere we went. We made day jumps, we made night jumps, we learned about a variety of weapons; and, spent a good deal of time on the target range.

One morning at 0600 we were mustered out with packs and rifles and began a three mile march to a nearby lake. North Carolina is known for its mild winters–well this was not one of them. It was about 15° out, you can imagine how we all felt. Our commander, a man named Captain Warfield, was one tough guy–but fair with all of us. He was a good leader. At the lake he kept marching and walked right in, clothes and all, saying, "Follow me across!" This is when we all thought he had flipped his lid. We thought, "That water is cold!" But we all followed him right into the lake and started across.

We devised our shelter haves (which is one half of a pup tent, buttoned together along the top) with our rifles so they floated in the shelter half and we, with Mae West's (which was the common name of our floatation vests), practically swam across the lake. When we reached the other side, about a quarter of a mile swim, our clothes began to instantly freeze on us as soon as we were out of the water. Captain Warfield's idea for keeping warm was to double-time it back to the barracks. As soon as we got there we all took hot showers to try and warm up.

Several nights after this polar bear experience we lined up for a night jump. This was always exciting, but most of us were very apprehensive. That night we jumped at a place called Andy's Field. It was only a short field and had an awful lot of trees. Considering the darkness, the jump came off very

13

well.  As we were all gathering up our chutes and heading off to the trucks for the ride back to Bragg, we heard someone calling for help.  We stopped and heard it again.  Not wanting to ignore a buddy that may need assistance, we went to locate the caller.

Now, in the service you have some fellas that don't always get along too well with the unit.  This happened to be one of them–an old sergeant no one seemed to have much to do with.  He was caught way up in the tree.  We called out, "Who is it?"  He yelled down to us, "Sergeant Hammer!"  Well, we decided to leave him hanging and headed off for the trucks.  Next morning we are all standing outside, lined up, when down the road came the sergeant–cursing and fuming.  "I've been up in a tree all night and last night someone came by and asked who I was...I told them, and they kept on going and left me hanging!"  Poor Sarge, he was tattered and torn and had a filthy face.  When he got a little closer we all put our heads down and laughed about it.  Even our lieutenant, Henry Keep had all he could do to keep from laughing at the sight of the sergeant.

Some mornings when we would fall out it would be so cold, we were instructed to button the top button on our coveralls.  Then we would start jogging all the way around Pope Airfield–this is only about 15 miles.  Now some guys would drop out at various distances.  We were always told to rest and then continue on, trying to catch up.  Our Company Commander, Captain Warfield, was sure proud of our unit.  He entered us in different endurance contests.  He had us jogging long distances over hills and through wooded areas.  Proudly, we usually came in first place.  We were always treated well for winning these contests, freely issuing us passes to get off the base.  We made him look good and both he and the company made a name for themselves.

One day we got word of a special assignment–a jump on Myrtle Beach in South Carolina. Everybody was fired up and excited about this jump. Myrtle Beach had a reputation as a summer, elite vacation spot. So we thought this would be nice to jump among the tourists. We flew down the coast and out over the ocean, coming back toward the beach we jumped. We returned to base by truck. We were going through some pretty thick woods; and, of all things, we found a baby pig! You just can't leave good pork in the woods so back to Bragg it came with us. This little fella was a great pet. Everyday most of us brought food back from the mess hall and fed him–he got big! He was a great pet, kept all the stray dogs away from our area. For some reason that pig couldn't tolerate dogs around our barracks. We had him tied up in the center of our area on a pole. This cute little guy was secured between the wooden framed barracks. Our little friend seemed quite content. Sadly, before we went overseas, we had a barbeque in which our friend was the guest of honor. You know, for some reason, not many of the guys were very hungry.

One of our platoon leaders, a second lieutenant, was from Pittsburgh, Pennsylvania. His family was well-to-do, they apparently had a lot of stock in Pittsburgh Steel. One day he noticed that we sure waited a long time for buses to get into town. Fayettville was about ten miles away and the city buses were our only means of transportation. One day the lieutenant was in town and he up and buys a brand new Buick. According to what we heard, the lieutenant walked onto the showroom floor and shelled out cash for his new black 1942 Buick. He said we could all use it for trips to town whenever we wanted.

The Buick was used many a night to go Charlie hunting. Charlie you see had a tremendous taste for beer. We often found ourselves going from one Fayettville tavern to the next till we found Charlie. It usually didn't take too long to find him. Two of us would go in, and with one of us on each side of Charlie, we'd literally drag him out to the Buick. Upon getting him back to the barracks we'd throw Charlie right in the shower, clothes and all, and then we'd put him to bed. Yell...he sure could holler at us. Next day he never knew what took place the night before. Charlie was really a wonderful guy–he was our platoon's sniper. Charlie grew up in a rural area where he developed his shot by doing a lot of hunting–he was a very good marksman.

The times seemed to bring out the very best in some people. When you were lucky enough to get some time off, Lieutenant Henry would always make sure you had enough money to cover the fare home and a little extra just for spending money. He was very generous toward the men in the company. I fondly remember his generosity and kindness. One Saturday night he threw a company party, a big dance with all the trimmings, snacks and soft drinks for everyone. He had several loads of girls brought in from the local college. The lieutenant arranged for trucks to transport the girls to the base and then back again to their school. We got the trucks all cleaned up and made sure the girls had benches to sit on.

Lieutenant Henry was in a class by himself. He was the most generous person I had ever seen or met. On one occasion, just before we all went overseas, we were going to hold a uniform inspection. They wanted to make sure no buttons were missing, no rips in the clothes or any tears. All the replacement clothes any of us needed were paid for by the lieutenant. He always seemed to go above and beyond for us–no matter what it cost him. Before we left to go overseas, Lieutenant Keep gave the Buick as a gift to another lieutenant, so his wife would have some transportation while we were gone.

Once during our stint at Fort Bragg, Lieutenant Henry invited all the officers in our company to his home in Pennsylvania for a weekend. We couldn't wait to ask them what their weekend was like. From what we all heard upon their return, they had a wonderful time. No one wanted to

17

come back to Bragg.

We also had a group that went to town one night, got liquored up, and came back with some tattoos. One joker in particular, Greg, had a large parachute tattooed on his leg with our unit's number 504th. Later, when we got the word we were going to be shipping out, we had to take all emblems and insignias off our clothes. The secrecy of the times is hard to understand today, but the army did not want anyone to know our unit was shipping out. We were mighty proud—we were going to be the first United States Army Airborne unit to ever see a fight on foreign soil. The first American parachute troops to see combat! Well, our proud friend, Greg, with the parachute tattoo on his leg, was in no uncertain terms told to get the tattoo removed or the Company Commander would personally cut it off his leg. Greg quickly had the tattoo changed so you would never know it was a parachute. In fact, it now resembled a girl holding an umbrella!

Another bad habit that some of the guys had was to make themselves drinks using vanilla extract. Now vanilla might not be bad to mix in cookies or cake, but drinking that stuff made some guys goofy. They would steal the bottles from the mess hall and hide the bottles in their shoes. These guys would volunteer for mess hall duty whenever their supply would run low, just to get their hands on the vanilla. Only a few men were involved in this...thank God.

Now we were busily involved in getting ready to head overseas, getting all our gear in good shape. During this time I wrote home and told the family that we were quarantined because we were preparing to ship out. I wrote my older sister, Ann, to tell her we were not able to see anyone. She didn't listen. She insisted on coming all the way down from St. Paul, Minnesota to North Carolina on the train. When she arrived in April of 1943, she was told no one could come out of the Fort; and, definitely, no one was going in. She was very disappointed and in her distress she turned to the Red Cross. They too told her there was nothing they could do to help her or intervene. Ann even tried telephoning me, but all to no avail. In disgust she returned to St. Paul without seeing or speaking to me. Even my officers said they could do nothing about it–they too were sorry Ann had traveled over a thousand miles to see me, but the war came first. I was not alone in this experience. Others too had family and friends arrive and found the situation the same as Ann.

We were now placed on alert. We could be shoving off anytime–this only made the situation more hectic. Everyone was nervous. Yet, we were all excited, this is why we had gone through all the training of the last nine months. The anticipation of seeing the war first-hand would make anyone excited. Before leaving we had a big feast of barbecued ribs with all the beer we could drink. A good time was had by all.

# SAILING AWAY

In late April of 1943 we took our gear and hopped aboard a troop train for an unknown destination. We rode this train for several days and finally found out that we were going to Camp Edwards in Massachusetts. Camp Edwards, who had ever heard of that before? To this day I still don't know where Camp Edwards is located. The shutters on the train had to be kept closed through the entire trip–security was definitely tight.

We arrived at Camp Edwards on Good Saturday, the day before Easter. Not even having settled into the new barracks, the following morning several of us figured we should go to church. Not knowing anything about the Camp or the area, we headed out the gate and on down the road in the direction of some church-bells. We got there just before the service started and marched right up the aisle to the first pew. The bunch of us were Catholics so we figured it would be a good idea if we all went to communion. You know, things seemed a bit odd. As the service progressed we took note that some things were a bit different than what we were used to, but we weren't familiar with how they held church in Massachusetts. Just to be on the safe side, we all left just a little early, later finding out that we had been in an Episcopal church. Everyone sure got a laugh out of that experience.

We no sooner arrived at Camp Edwards than we were shipping out–we only stayed the weekend. It was back on the train to our port of embarkation, New York. It was about midnight when we got into New York. As we got off the train there were two lines of secret service agents that flanked us from the train to the gang plank. These guys kept cautioning us to move quickly and move quietly. As we went up to the ship we passed under a huge arch which read, "Through these portals pass the best damn soldiers in the world." At the same time we were being hurried on to the ship and told to be quiet, an army band was playing *Over There.* It was one heck of a feeling–thinking about how we got this far so soon.

The ship was the George Washington, a former German vessel. It was so crowded that half of us had to sleep down below at night for the first half of the trip; and, top-side for the last half. We didn't know if this was good or bad. But during the night when we were below deck we could hear explosions which was awful scary. In the morning we would go up on deck and ask the sailors what the noise was during the night. The sailors would point to all the oil in the water and explain how the destroyers were dropping depth charges during the night, successfully sinking two submarines. During the day it wasn't any quieter. The ship's crew would have anti-aircraft practice and would allow us to man the 20mm guns on the deck. Practice took place each day for about an hour--the noise from these guns was ear-shattering.

We were traveling in a convoy of about twenty ships. The destroyers were on the outside and next to us on the inside was a huge ship–the Battleship Texas. It carried a small sea-plane on board and each day for at least an hour it would be sent aloft in search of German submarines. This continued until one day while the plane was landing, a swell opened up next to the Texas and the plane flipped over on its back with the pilot flying out. A destroyer was called over. After rescuing the pilot they fired a shell into the plane and sunk it. We learned later that the convoy could not be stopped for anything--this included salvaging the plane. While on board the ship we tried to keep busy–and there always seemed to be something going on. Standing in lines consumed a lot of time, like standing in chow line and standing at the P.X. to buy cigarettes and candy. We learned quickly that you had to be very careful about smoking at night. You took a real chance of getting shot on deck for doing such a foolish thing as smoking at night. You also never wanted to throw anything over the side–nothing even as small as a match. Anything thrown over the side could possibly be detected by a German submarine. And the Nazi submarines were all around our convoy.

We did have a large school of porpoises following our ship. They were there day and night, always looking for food. Late at night the kitchen crew would open the side doors of the ship and throw the garbage over the side. The porpoises loved it and cleaned up any trail of the convoy.

During the last half of the trip my group slept on the deck. We felt if we got hit with a torpedo at night we could jump over the side rather than suffer down below. The entire trip was made by the convoy zig-zagging across the ocean. It was hoped that if a torpedo did come our way that we would zig instead of zag and cause the torpedo to miss its intended target.

# CASABLANCA

As I recall, it was May of 1943 when we finally arrived at Casablanca. We could all smell something like incense and everyone seemed to shout in unison, "Take us back to the States." Our ship was taken into the harbor by the harbor pilot. We were all standing on one side of the ship to get a good look at the city and we were causing the ship to list. We were asked to even it up so the pilot could get the ship to shore.

On the shore were thousands of native and French Africans, little kids and grown-ups, greeting us. We disembarked down the gang plank and lined up in formation before marching ten miles out of town.

The gravel road to our camp was dry and dusty. Morocco seemed to be rather flat with little scenery. As we marched we were permitted to smoke. All along the way we were flanked by little Arab kids. Whenever we flicked a cigarette butt it no sooner hit the ground the kids would snatch them up.

We put up our pup tents in rows and settled down into our new home. Our camp was a flat, sandy field approximately the size of an acre, covered with our tents. On either side of the tents we dug slit trenches for protection. These trenches were about one and a half to two feet wide and about two to three feet deep. Most of us dug them eight feet long. We established a perimeter, an imaginary line, about 200 feet from our tents. On all four corners we set up water-cooled, machine guns. Believe me, there were Arabs by the hundreds standing at our imaginary line. These people had everything in the world to sell. There were loads of eggs, cucumbers, tomatoes and wine. If they didn't have it–they would get it.

Some of the guys bought wine. One of the fellas started in on his bottle and got goofy as could be. He went to

23

the ammo pile and took a case of hand grenades, pulling the pins and throwing them all over the area. You talk about people jumping into slit trenches in a hurry or anywhere else to be safe. Our executive officer, Lieutenant Wilson, ran at him shouting for him to stop throwing the grenades before he killed or seriously injured someone. But every time he threw a grenade, the officer dove into a slit trench. After the explosion he would jump up and run toward the guy again. Finally he got to the soldier and brought a stop to the dangerous *fun* he was having. The lieutenant had him taken to our field hospital, a big tent within our camp, for treatment. The medics had to strap him down in bed until he sobered up. They found what was left of the bottle and analyzed the contents. Among other things it contained shoe dye and coloring. Needless to say, Lieutenant Wilson was one heck of an officer and was he furious at the Arabs.

In our tent area we had all sorts of ammunition, enough to fill a full-size railroad box-car. We were told to take all we wanted to practice. Everyday we fired mortar shells, rifles, T.N.T., anything we wanted for practice. Before firing the mortars we would post signs, *Danger-shelling taking place*. If anyone went up into the hills, they went up there at their own risk. We also enjoyed blowing up buildings using the quarter pound blocks of T.N.T. These were empty, isolated buildings in the desert, made mostly of mud and stone. We would place a charge at each corner of a building and set it off. What an explosion that would cause. Target shooting was done a lot. We would use every weapon that we had available: the mortars, machine guns, rifles and bazookas. During our stay outside Casablanca we also did a lot of bayonet practice, both day and night, to keep our skills sharp.

On occasion we would get passes to go into Casablanca. The streets were for the most part paved, and about as wide as a normal street found throughout America. But the stench was something we couldn't get used to. There were no sanitary sewers–the toilet water just ran out into the street. The structures in Casablanca came in every shape and size, but most of the buildings had flat roofs. People dressed in a variety of ways, as they do in America today. Some modern and some in traditional garb of long robes.

We always went into Casablanca in groups of two or three because you never knew what you would run into in town. We always kept our eye peeled for *Humphrey Bogart* or *Ricks,* but never saw either one. One day Sergeant Bill White, who hailed from Arkansas and was perpetually kidded by all of us about swinging on vines; Al Bigeon, who was from Boston, and I, headed into town. The three of us were all newly promoted sergeants. The three of us seemed to hang out a lot together. We saw what appeared to be a liquor shop, but to our surprise and disappointment turned out to be a perfume store. Sometimes it was hard to tell what a particular shop was selling. The smell of freshly baked goods brought us to what we thought was going to be a bakery--to our pleasant surprise it was. We went in and had a heck of time trying to understand the proprietor and he us. We finally got a huge bag of some simple, plain, sugar cookies. Unfortunately, we were caught in the act. As we turned to leave we found about fifty kids staring at us through the window. As soon as we got out the door we were surrounded by these street urchins with their hands out. Well we got rid of the bag of cookies right there.

One day, we came across what appeared to be a nice restaurant and decided to have lunch. Once again, we had a terrible time trying to communicate and understand the locals. We finally got it across to them that we would like to try the chicken. The chicken was baked and it wasn't so bad--we all had our fill. What really shocked us was the bill--$16 for the three of us. That was about twice what we would expect to pay at home in those days. And today, three can eat at the Colonel's for less than that! 

Strolling through Casablanca we came upon a bicycle stand and decided we would see more of the city by riding.

We each rented a bike. These were your typical one speed, brake-pedal type bikes with skinny tires. We thought we were off for a tour of Casablanca. To our surprise, Al couldn't ride a lick. We soon discovered this after he smashed the bike into a stone wall and ruined the front wheel. That was the end of the bike ride. Al paid for his damages and we walked from then on.

During these trips to Casablanca I saw things that reminded me I was no longer in St. Paul, Minnesota. Mothers would be just walking down the street while nursing their babies. Another reminder of being far from home was the smell. Some of the streets had just a horrible smell since the sewer in each building was simply piped into the street gutters. We also ran into a lot of French soldiers who were waiting for new orders or had just returned from the fighting in North Africa. A lot of people were begging on the street and the French soldiers would chase the beggars away.

While in Casablanca we also visited a few of their bars. Moroccan bars or taverns were similar to those back home. They all seemed to have long wooden bars, lots of ceiling fans and the assorted tables and chairs for patrons to gather around. Wherever we went we found French soldiers. Their favorite beverages seemed to be cognac or wine.

You couldn't escape the beggars in a bar either–they were there with their hands out. Most of the beggars we ran across were Arab and they did not get along with any of the French soldiers.

Something that really surprised and amazed us were the bathrooms. They did not distinguish between men or women like in the States. There were no commodes either, just a simple hole or two in the floor. You had to be a pretty good aim, and sober, to hit the hole. You could be in the toilet relieving yourself and a woman would come in and squat down and do the same. When that happened I got out of there in a hurry. Another missing ingredient was toilet paper. From the tell-tale signs on the walls, people mostly used their fingers or whatever they had to finish the job.

One day one of our guys was missing from morning roll call. We loaded up several jeeps with four guys in each. We armed ourselves with tommy guns and went into Casablanca to look for him. After searching for a while we found him in an alley with his throat cut. Two guys, who we assumed had done this, since the locals were pointing at them and shouting, were running away. They got up on a rooftop and as they were running on the rooftops we all started firing our machine guns these two guys. This sort of action did not happen too often. We were constantly being cautioned to never go into Casablanca alone–always in twos or threes for safety sake.

At our camp, some Arabs dressed in long robes or gowns with turbans and some dressed in slacks and shirts. They would come and stand at the perimeter line all day long, either to buy or sell. We took our mattress covers which were plain cotton, pull-on, slip-covers much like a large pillow case; rolled them up under our arms and went out to make a deal. We would stand there showing them the covers and telling them, "Mattress cover." The Arabs would show us their money and would fight each other to buy the cover. We usually got around $25 for a mattress cover. (And we questioned our government over $700 toilet seats a few years ago.) The Arabs would cut a hole in the top end and two holes in the sides and pull them over their heads to wear like a gown. Were they ever proud of those mattress cover-gowns! This got to be pretty good, so we cut a couple of them in half. The Arabs bought them, sight unseen. They would take them and run over the hill to look at their purchase. There they would find out that they had been had. They came right back crying and holding up the half covers and shouting in French. Sometimes we gave them some money back. But from then on they were very careful to check before consummating the deal, to see if they were buying a whole cover or just a half.

The Arabs were salesmen too. They would come with baskets full of eggs–plain, white chicken eggs. We used a lot of eggs, frying them up in our mess kits. We would take the eggs and pay the Arabs what we thought they were worth. We tried to be fair with them. They had all sorts of vegetables too, especially cucumbers and tomatoes. To understand how much we appreciated the Arab eggs and vegetables, you have know that we had been living on C-rations. We were getting extremely tired of eating them since they only seemed to come in three varieties: meat and beans; potato hash; and stew. After a while they all tasted the same.

Some of the Arabs had horses–Arabian horses of course. The Arabs would stand at the perimeter with their saddled horses. We had never seen such saddles--each one appeared to have been home-made. To determine the length of a ride, we would point to the sun in the sky, and then where it would be when we would return from our ride. Well, we would ride all over the place. These horses were beautiful animals. Could they run! They would scare you at the speeds they could go. We all took turns until everyone had all they could take of riding. Then we would just turn the horses loose. No matter, the next day there were the Arabs with their horses again. These horses must have made their way back home all by themselves.

One evening we figured we would have a little fun at the Arabs expense. They were all standing around the perimeter, our imaginary line, with all their wares. Out in the desert it was dark. We took our rifles and fixed our bayonets. We crawled out almost to the Arabs, then jumped up and yelled as loud as we could and came at them. We went for the ones with the eggs. I believe they thought we had all gone berserk and they began to run away like the devil was after them. We got an awful lot of eggs like that.

While in camp, Lieutenant Henry Keep and Captain Warfield kept their distance from us, especially during our business dealings with the Arabs. After helping Lieutenant

Keep set up his tent and arrange things for him, he gave us a white bed sheet for helping him. So we took the sheet out and showed it to the Arabs. As soon as they saw it they started fighting among themselves and began bidding on it. They all wanted that sheet. It sold for $50.

I was running out of things to sell so I took a look through my barracks bag to see what I may have in there to offer. I came up with a set of long, woolen, Army-green, winter, underwear, the one-piece kind with the trap door, and a pair of rubber overshoes with buckles up the front. In Africa it was about 115° to 120° so I didn't really need them. I took them out to the line and showed the Arabs what I had. The bidding began and I eventually sold them. Low and behold, next morning there was the Arab who had bought my offering standing in line wearing the long underwear and overshoes. This was a sight to behold. We all must have laughed for an hour. Oh how we wished we had a camera. A picture like that would have been worth a fortune.

One day we were told to get ready to make a jump for General Dwight Eisenhower, British Prime Minister Winston Churchill and a number of other dignitaries including General Matthew Ridgeway who headed up the First Allied Airborne Army which included our 504th Paratrooper Infantry Regiment. The First Allied Airborne Army was composed of one United States Division, one British Division and one from our brothers to the north, a Canadian Division.

The purpose for this jump was to demonstrate what a combat jump would be like. First the bombers flew over. There must have been about fifty. There were B-24's and B-17's. They were followed by about seventy-five P-51 fighter planes. One of the commanders designated our landing zone in a field strewn with large rocks. When we jumped one of the fellas, a sergeant, got injured on landing. He hit his head, protected by his helmet liner, on a rock. His regular, steel, helmet was not available since it was in for repair. This screwed up his sight. He had double-vision. Whenever he looked at anyone he would see two, one on top of the other. During his stay in the hospital on our base we would visit him everyday and help him write letters home because when he tried to write he went off the paper every time. There was nothing the medical personnel could do for him so he was sent back to Johns Hopkins in the States.

When we weren't selling to the Arabs, we were actively involved in our training and preparation for combat. Whenever you are on the rifle range and experience a malfunction, you immediately take the weapon to one of the ordinance officers. Well one of the guys had a problem with his rifle and he set it down by the ordinance men who were busy at the time with other weapons. Just about the same time, the fellas on guard duty began loading up the trucks to head back to camp. One of the ordinance officers took this rifle and began to check it out to see what was wrong with it. He released the bolt and the rifle went off, striking a man on the truck who was going back to camp for guard duty. The round went right through the cap of his canteen and into his side–killing him. Tragedies like this seemed to happen occasionally as we prepared to face the Germans. On another occasion we were training with our bayonets. While working our way through barbed wire entanglements, one of the fellows, Joe, got caught by the seat of his pants in the barbed wire. It spun him around and he fatally fell on his own bayonet, which pierced him in the side. Considering the numbers of young men training with live ammunition, grenades and bayonets in a variety of conditions, like jumping out of airplanes, the casualties were very low.

Preparations were soon under way for leaving the Casablanca area. We were to be headed further east to a town called Oujda in French Morocco. We were to travel by train and Sergeant Bill Smith and I were in charge of the guards. We learned that if we kept our noses clean throughout training, rank such as sergeant came easily.

While waiting in the Casablanca train station we saw

a couple of companies of French Senegalese, very tall, black soldiers. In the heat of Africa these soldiers were wearing overcoats with the front corners tied up to give their legs freedom to move. They were very curious and interested in our M-1 rifle. The Senegalese were issued old French single shot rifles. Easy to see why they liked our M-1 rifles better. Their English was not very good. For example, as a French officer rode by on a horse, the Senegalese pointed at him and called the horse a jeep.

Bill and I made an inspection of all the box cars before we loaded up. All of the cars had been cleaned up for the troops. Bill and I got to ride in a box car designated as our supply car including all the food. Once we were loaded and underway, Bill and I unrolled our Army issue bed-rolls, a type of sleeping bag, on top of a large shipment of wooden cases containing all sorts of food stuff. During the trip we had access to anything we wanted.

Our car had several windows on each side, just some square holes in the wooden walls, and we would just lay there watching the scenery roll by. We discovered a large tin, about twenty-five pounds, of hard candy. Every town we passed through the kids would just swarm around the crossings as the train slowed through town and Bill and I would throw hand-fulls of candy to these kids. They would just about kill one another to get a piece of candy. This went on for town after town. We never saw so many kids. How they all knew we were coming was beyond us.

During our two-day trip, Bill and I got in some target practice. We shot out the windows at anything and everything we saw. We had it pretty nice in our car, everything from all the food we could want, to candy for the kids to target practice whenever we felt like it. In scrounging around in the car we found a special treat--a large can of cocoa. Bill and I enjoyed a whole day of pouring down chocolate drinks. We had a G.I. can of water, one of the five gallon type, and we used this to mix our chocolate.

31

When our regiment, the 504th, arrived in Oujda we all disembarked and were driven to an olive orchard about fifteen miles out from the actual town of Oujda. The orchard we camped in was about two blocks long and just as wide. This was a great place to pitch camp, every tent was under a tree. These olive trees were pretty old, most were about ten to fifteen feet in diameter and only about fifteen feet high. We could only guess at how long this particular orchard had been there. In this desert heat we needed the shade. Another reason the Army choose this orchard was the impregnable hedge that surrounded it. The bushes comprising this hedge were about ten feet high and so thick a dog couldn't chase a rabbit through it. Each of the four sides of the hedge had an opening where we posted a guard twenty-four hours a day. It was so warm during the day that the officers choose to conduct all our training at night. During the day we did whatever we wanted, but mostly tried to stay comfortable while getting a little shut-eye.

While camping near Oujda we were only issued one canteen of water a day. This was horrible. In this extreme heat we all needed more than that. Bill, Al and I decided to check out the area around our camp. We made a wonderful discovery–an Arab farmer who used an ox and a camel for an irrigation team. This fella was busy raising cucumbers, lettuce and tomatoes in his garden. He was driving the team forward down a slope, opposite a well where he drew the water and the team pulled up a large leather bag full of water. When the bag got to the top of the slope it would spill out into a large trough. We checked his well, which was completely concealed by some heavy brush and figured this water had to be okay. Being ever ready, we had our jump ropes with us. Jump ropes are about twenty-five feet long and all paratroopers carry them to have on hand should you need to dislodge yourself from a tree upon landing. We put our jump ropes to good use. We tied them to our helmets and lowered our steel helmets into the well, drawing out the sweet, cool

32

water. We were sure glad we only had helmets to shade our heads from the sun–a straw hat would not have done us much good. We drank our fill, right from our helmets. We all noticed a few bugs in the water, but this didn't bother us, we figured the bugs were thirsty too and they didn't drink much.

Everyday we visited the well. The farmer was quite friendly, but we never did get his name. While he was filling his trough, we would stand under the water bags and let them soak us, coveralls and all. He did not seem to mind us getting wet with his water and it sure felt good. This Arab's field was no more than a city block from our camp. After we got our fill of water and were sufficiently soaked, we would head back to camp. The desert is so hot and so dry, with a scorching wind, that by the time we got back to camp we were dry as a bone. While camped at Oujda we saw very few Arabs, other than our farmer friend; and, we never really missed them.

This cruel desert didn't allow too much to grow other than a few scrub bushes, some cacti and trees like those in our olive orchard camp. It seemed like the hot, dry breeze never stopped blowing. The farmer's well took care of *our* water, the camp got its *official* water about ten miles away, from some place called Holy City. It was so flat in our part of the desert that you could stand in our camp and see all the way to Holy City. In the heat it would be waving on the horizon.

Next to our camp was the airfield. The pilots often asked us if we wanted to ride along with them as they were getting in their flying time. It was a treat that we always enjoyed. The planes were A20 light bombers. The pilots would always try to get us to sit in the nose turret. That's because they had a mean streak in them. They could sure scare the heck out of you by diving straight down toward the ocean and then pull up just a few feet from the water. It didn't take us long to figure that one out, and we refused to ride in the nose. We also got to go up in the C47's. The pilots always appreciated some company while they were putting in their flying time.

It seems like our outfit always had some kind of animal for a pet–from our pig back at Bragg; to our monkey and a little jackass, Beanie, that we found in Oujda. Every time a jeep would start up, that monkey was right there hanging on to the windshield. He loved to go for jeep rides. But when we got ready to leave Oujda, we couldn't find the monkey–he must have just wandered off.

We had to carry a lot of equipment when we jumped: mortars, shells, and machine guns. Naturally, we were always looking for an easy way to get a job done. And one day we figured out how we could get out of carrying all the equipment. We visited the parachute riggers and asked them to make a harness for Beanie, and indeed they did. Now, here we are with a parachute for the jackass, so the company commander, Captain Warfield, told us we had to go up and jump with Beanie to see if everything would be okay. We arranged for the jump. Beanie was a white-knuckle flyer and we all had to pitch in to push Beanie out the door. Once that mission was accomplished we went right out after him. Everything was going great until Beanie looked down and grasped the fact that the ground was rushing up to meet him. Poor thing stiffened his legs and when he hit the ground you could hear his legs breaking. We did the most humane thing we could for him–shot him. Hindsight is wonderful. If we only knew, we would have blindfolded him so he would not be able to see the ground. Being more relaxed, Beanie just may have made it as a "para-jackass". We were not going to give up so easy, which lead to our scouring the area for another jackass, but we had no luck. Can't you just see a plane loaded with paratroops and a jackass. As this contingent was coming down from the sky you'd probably run for your life, wondering what the war was coming to. We missed Beanie, he sure would have been a big help in lugging all the heavy equipment.

While in Oujda there were times when some of the guys would ride the water trucks to Holy City. It was forbidden for anyone to wander around in Holy City, we were never told why, just get the water and get out. The water was put in Lister bags. These are large canvas bags that hold about thirty gallons of water. We hung them back at camp on tripods. The Lister bags always seemed to be hanging around in the sun, never in the shade, so the water was always hot.

One of the strangest things to happen when we were in camp at Oujda happened in the chow-line of all places. A couple of German stragglers/deserters in G.I. uniform were discovered in our food line. Nobody really ever talked while they in were in line, we all just kind of shuffled along and gathered up our C-rations. Boy, was that a surprise when the Germans were found!

On the morning the company was scheduled to go swimming in the Mediterranean I was among several of us who missed morning reveille. Our punishment was to roll equipment bundles with rocks. The planes were going to drop them that night while we were out training. The punishment turned out in our favor. Just about every last man returned from their day at the sea burnt to a crisp from all the sun and salt water. Their backs were so badly burned they had to carry their loaded packs in their hands. When the planes came over and dropped the bundles we had rolled all day, we told the fellas that some of those bundles aren't tied very well. Some of them didn't know which way to run. After none of the bundles came apart they all realized we were just kidding.

During the daytime we did a little shooting practice and just sort of lounged around. It was just too hot to do anything else. As hot as it was during the day, at night it was just the opposite. We found ourselves often wearing our medium weight, field jackets just to stay warm and ward off the desert night chill. The weather in north Africa is something that none of us ever got used to.

In our travels around the area we discovered a couple of discontinued wells that were full of brand new jeep and truck tires. These were American tires. Who threw them in and where they got them in the first place was only conjecture on our part.  Sure made us wonder, since back in the States you could not buy tires due to the war effort.  The war had already gone through this area and raised all kinds of heck. The tires may have been dumped by some American unit when it was on the move.

We knew something was afoot because all kinds of rumors were circulating.  There was a lot of talk about the Italians.  We heard that their soldiers used "dumb-dumb" bullets.  These were fearful rounds that would tear a fella to pieces inside if he got hit with one.  Some of our guys were saying that if you caught an Italian and they had "dumb-dumb" bullets that we should just shoot 'em in the back with their own bullets.  We also heard that the Germans had to chain the Italians to their own artillery pieces to keep them from running away.

One night the powers that be flew in a nice dinner for us–beef and turkey with all the trimmings and wine.  We joked about it because it kind of felt like they were serving us our last supper.  In some ways, and for some of our company, it was.  Having a nice dinner was special since we did not often have so much good food.

None of us knew for sure where we were going to invade.  We didn't find out that our target was Sicily until we were in the air.  It was kept a closely guarded secret.  There was no doubt, though, that something was up because they gathered up all our bayonets and sharpened them for us. Every night we were going through bayonet drill.  We had been told not to load our rifles before a combat jump but to wait until after we were on the ground.  After we hit the ground whose rear-end is being shot at anyway; and, whose rear-end are we trying to save?  I loaded my rifle and was prepared for whatever was out there.

# SICILY

## or

## (YOU'RE NOT IN ST. PAUL ANYMORE)

July 9, 1943, as I recall it was a Tuesday, the day we invaded Sicily. That evening we were all lying around on the tarmack, under the wings of the various planes we were assigned to for our jump. Lot's of courageous talk was going on. We were talking about how we were going to kick some German rear ends since we felt we were well trained and prepared for the fight that lay ahead. We boldly spoke of how we would use our bayonets on those guys. There was no doubt among us that we would all be back in Africa in just a few days for some rest. Some of us were nervous, but none us wanted to show it. We just didn't know what to expect or what was about to happen.

We all figured we had plenty of ammo to get our job done. We were loaded down with everything we thought we would need once we got on the ground: pockets full of hand grenades, we each carried at least ten; about ten clips of bullets, each clip had eight rounds in it; two bandoliers with additional rounds, bringing each man's total to about 200 rounds of ammunition. We also carried the Soldier's Prayer Book, a non-denominational book of scripture and prayers; toilet paper and cigarettes. Topping off the equipment list was our reserve parachute and our regular or main chute.

The jump-master, Cliff, a master sergeant who had been in the Army for about ten years, read off the names and your jump number, the assigned position inside the plane. At first I was way back in the plane. Then a jeep drove up at the last minute with a rigger in it who said he was assigned to our plane. Everyone was going on the invasion--even the support personnel. So Cliff assigned the rigger to the rear of the plane in my spot and I was assigned number three which is just across from the open door–a perfect spot. Thank God for that favor, as this rigger was the first casualty on our plane. He was blown right out of his seat when the anti-aircraft fire began...this could have been me. Just not my time. The Good Lord had all kinds of other ideas and experiences awaiting me over the course of the next couple of years.

We left the Oujda airfield one plane at a time and rendezvoused in the air for the flight to Sicily once all the planes were lined up. There were about forty planes in this operation with anywhere between twenty-five and thirty-five men per plane. There were slightly less than 1,000 of us assigned to this spearhead operation and I was on the lead plane. Until we took off, the rest of the operation was standing at the ready. As the *Berlin Bitch*[2] said, they had ground for each of us–six feet of it–meaning, no survivors. We headed out over the Mediterranean for our two hour flight into hell. On the flight we were re-assigned our new name, the "X Battalion of the 505th," commanded by Colonel Rubin Tucker, with General Matthew Ridgeway in charge of the operation.

We were the spear-head of the invasion of Sicily–the Allies first foot-hold in Europe. We were going to be the first American paratroopers to be tried in combat and to jump into hostile conditions on foreign soil. From a newspaper clipping that my dad had saved for me, that I finally read after the war, I learned there were twenty-three planes in the first wave. The rest of our Unit, the 504th, was scheduled to arrive the next day; but many were lost to friendly fire while crossing the Mediterranean.

We had been assured that it was going to be a dark night. Who were those weather forecasters anyway? It was anything but dark! The moon was out and it was shining about as bright as ever. We also wondered if we would ever

---

2      The Berlin Bitch was a female radio announcer in Germany who broadcast to the Allied soldiers.

get over the drop zone since we were encountering winds of about 40 mph. The flight was not smooth, we were being bounced around and began to wonder how far off course we were being blown.

We knew as soon as we were over Sicily because the anti-aircraft fire was unbelievable. It was something else. As the plane bounced along, we did our best to stay put in our seats which were no more than small aluminum trays fastened to the fuselage. We just hung onto anything we could to stay put. The flack was so thick I think the pilot could have put the wheels down and driven on top of it. The anti-aircraft fire blew holes in the plane. I can recall at one point looking out through a hole in the bulkhead and seeing the moon.

As if this wasn't bad enough, the German shelling hit our starboard or right engine. I thank God it wasn't on the door-side. The engine on the left side of the plane seemed to be okay. The jump-door is on the left or port side of the plane as you are looking forward.

By this time the guys were being blown right out of their seats. The floor of the plane was already covered with bodies. Strange, but after months of training with these guys, I don't recall any of the names of those who were lying in the plane before we jumped. Those of us waiting to jump were not only scared, but we were getting angry–what were those Germans doing to us!? Of course, we were on our way to kill and destroy them, so I suppose reflecting back now, I can understand what they were doing. There was plenty of fear to go around in the plane as we waited for the jump signal. But it was sort of surreal–there was no real panic.

After what seemed like an eternity to those of us still lucky enough to have dodged the shell with our name on it, the pilot turned on the light that signaled us to stand up and prepare to jump. Cliff, our jump-master, some other fellas, and I hooked up our static lines. The plane was really going wild by now–rolling and pitching all over...so many of our guys in the plane had already been hit or killed. When we got the green light–out the door we went. Thank God the door engine was alright.

Cliff yelled, "Let's get out of here while we can." I was so relieved to get out of that flying disaster. We could not have been much over 100 feet high when we bailed out, for just as my chute popped open my feet were scratching grass. Our plane fared no better than most of the soldiers, for as soon as we were out the door it flew straight into a nearby rocky outcrop of mountains. As for Cliff, I never saw him again, and have no idea what became of him.

After landing I just laid there on the ground. A couple of German machine guns were firing in my direction, raking the ground–combing the whole area where I landed–just a foot over my head. Back and forth they swept the entire area and then would repeat the maneuver. They were persistent and did not let up or cease firing for a long time. We must have landed in the midst of the German Army because there was shooting going on all around. I crawled for what felt like a mile, staying as low as I possibly could without burrowing into the ground. I was a good distance away from the machine guns anyway. At the same time we were being shelled by our own Navy! Those big 16 inch guns were pounding the area and we were on the receiving end. Those guns practically turned the island upside-down. Every time one of those shells landed it would lift you off the ground and throw you into the air about a foot.

I ran into two others guys in a field near some heavy bushes, Tony and Len, and later we found John. They too were from "I" Company of the 504th and had been on another plane in the operation. The three of us were walking along when we heard someone calling for help. We inched up to him and when we saw him we knew this guy was in pain. He told us that his leg had gotten caught up in the equipment bundle just as the equipment bundle parachute opened up. We depend upon these equipment bundles for our mortars, machine guns, bazookas and extra ammunition–but we never thought this could happen. The force of the chute opening had snapped the large shin bone. When we found this fella his shinbone looked like a hand-full of broom-straw sticking out of his boot. Our battalion was the only outfit to be issued morphine kits, we wore them strapped to our upper-right arm. This sure looked to me like a good time to put it to use. We had been instructed to be very careful using the syringes. Each of us had four morphine loads and one already in the syringe. I pulled one of mine out and gave him a shot to settle him down. Before you knew it he was quiet. Knowing we couldn't sit around with the area swarming with Germans, we dragged him under some bushes and told him to try and be quiet. Leaving him there we took off–the place was crawling with Germans.

The whole sky was lit up from the fire resulting from our plane crashing into a mountain. Our pilot was a big Texan, whose name we never knew, he had joked with us before we took off, "You boys know this is a one way ride." We told him just get us there and we'll do the rest. To this day I don't know if he got out before the crash, nothing could have survived the impact and fire.

Well, we had several skirmishes with the Germans during the night. We couldn't keep away from them–the area was full of the enemy. At every turn we were running across small German patrols. These troops were the elite Hermann Göring Division. We had been told that these were hardened, hand-picked soldiers. They may have been an elite outfit to the Germans, but it wasn't long before we found out they had a real distaste for hand-to-hand combat at which they were not very good. We, on the other hand, really knew how to use our bayonets. There were now four of us: Tony, Len, John and me. We deftly made use of our bayonets, rifle-butts, daggers, fists and the occasional bullet to dispatch a number of Germans. These skirmishes were brief episodes–hit and run. We had to keep on the move throughout the night for everywhere we went we ran into more German troops.

A lot of our skirmishing took place in open fields, but on several occasions we had the cover of ditches. We surprised a company of Germans and found out that Tony, Len, John and I were much better shots than they. The four of us greatly reduced their ranks before we took off up a hill. Most of the fighting at night was hand-to-hand. After these fights we would high-tail it out of there, only to run into more Germans. After a few fights like that we felt pretty super, kind of invincible. It was them or us. The four of us began to wonder where the rest of our Army was. We never did find our unit as we seemed to be scattered all over the island. The wind and the anti-aircraft shelling had really spread everyone around.

In several of our skirmishes, we would exchange gun-fire and they would fire back with their eighty-eights, an artillery gun. In one of these enemy encounters during the night, John, won his hand-to-hand duel with a Kraut. But when John tried to get his bayonet out of the German, he must have hit the release because the bayonet stayed in the German when he fell. John just dropped his rifle and ran across the field screaming till an 88 hit him–there was nothing left of John.

Later we saw an airfield on top of a hill and decided to try and make our way to it. As we crept up a path, every so often we came across a candle burning in a tin can. We took no chances and gave them a very wide berth, not wanting to cast any shadows and not wanting to disturb the candles and tip off any guards.

When we got to the top of the hill it was dark and quiet. We saw the German's barracks about two hundred yards away and lo and behold, right in front of us–a German fighter plane! They had tried to conceal it under a camouflage netting. It just so happens that we had been lugging a bazooka around all night, that we had found in a torn up equipment bundle. The bad news was we only had one round of ammunition for it. After sizing up the plane we figured one round could disable it. We placed the shot into the bazooka and put the round squarely in the plane's engine block. The noise of firing that thing was deafening. About then all hell broke loose–lights came on all over and soldiers came pouring out of their barracks, running in all directions. They started heading in our direction and we took off down the hill as quick as we could. We could hear them yelling and knew they were looking for us, but luck was on our side this night.

We never stopped all night, we just kept moving. We couldn't stop–the Germans were everywhere. We were headed in no particular direction–just moving away from the sounds of shooting. No maps were needed, we were able to find Germans at every turn. In this area of Sicily they outnumbered us easily ten to one. Our objective, as it had been explained to us, was to get the Germans away from the shores. The landing was going to be taking place and it was our job to get the Germans away from the beach and keep them occupied. From what history tells us we must have done a good job–because the Army infantry, coming over by boat, landed successfully on the shores. From what Ross S. Carter, a member of our relief, the 504th, wrote in *Those Devils in Baggy Pants*, before jumping the night after us they had heard two rumors. The first was that we had done well; and the second, that we had been annihilated or killed in our planes or chutes.[3] Carter had heard right in both of those rumors.

Our skirmishing continued. These were quick hit and run fights. Some were over in seconds and some lasted twenty minutes to an hour. Most of the time we tried to use ditches for cover as opposed to being in the open fields. Because there were so many Germans, we were able to get the drop on them most of the time. Knowing we were vastly outnumbered kept us on the alert for them. It seems they too were looking for us, because there were other paratroopers all over the island. These soldiers of the Goring Division knew they were up against an elite outfit.

Whenever they could zero in on us, the Germans would fire their eighty-eights, a type of howitzer. And believe me, those eight-eights were powerful. The gunners would often zero in on one man–like poor John. Oh, we dreaded those devils. Another wicked weapon the Germans had was what we called the meat-grinder. This is a mortar with about ten or twelve mortar tubes in a circle. They fire the weapon using a dial and I mean it is really something. It just roars when they let it go. Can it cover an area?! The meat-grinder can cover an area the size of a football field when all the tubes are fired at once. It was a devastating machine with a lot of killing power. Boy, when the meat-grinder started growling we would hunt for a hole as quick as we could.

---

3       Ross S. Carter, *Those Devils in Baggy Pants*, (Mattituck, New York: Amereon House, Buccaneer Books, Inc., 1976), 16.

Jessica Stacy
2002

On the third day we ran into a fella named Captain Ely and two others, Don and Bill, from Company H. Were we glad to meet up with these three guys–now the three of us felt a little safer. Captain Ely led the way–looking for Germans. His plan was simple, find the Germans and make a stand, find out who was the better soldier. Most of the time we were walking in fields and through the rolling hills of Sicily. Many of the hillsides are green with vineyards. In the middle of what seemed nowhere we came upon a large, farm-house, sitting on the side of hill. As we approached the house all hell broke loose. They were trying to kill us as we walked up to the house. We returned fire, not knowing if a German patrol had holed up in the house or what we had run across. The shooting didn't last long and a group of Sicilians, all in Italian Army uniforms came out with their hands in the air, shouting, "Don't shoot! Don't shoot!" They were very poor soldiers by our account. The captain queried the folks about anyone else being in the house. One of the men, who appeared to be their spokesman, assured us that the house was now empty. Instead of checking the premises, the captain and the rest of us just started walking away. A shot rang out and hit Bill in the stomach. Without saying a word, the captain grabbed the group's spokesman by the hair, pulled his head back and cut his throat from ear to ear–almost cutting off his head. We tossed some grenades in the house and got out of there.

Hoping to run into more of our outfit, Captain Ely thought we ought to split up. Captain Ely and Don headed off in one direction, with Tony, Len and I going another. We never saw them again. The three of us must have run into five or six German patrols. There were usually five to seven Germans in a patrolling unit and we would have it out with them, always keeping on the move. In the dark of night we encountered a German patrol and started in on them with our bayonets. I got so close I got two fingers cut pretty good by a German's bayonet, but that was his last hostile act. The Germans proved to be pretty good soldiers, but we considered ourselves just a little bit better.  Whether we were engaging them in hand to hand combat or just shooting it out with them, we felt superior.

# THE VINEYARD

"Now I will tell you what I am going to do to my vineyard.
I will take away its hedge; and it will be destroyed.
I will break down its wall, and it will be trampled.
I will make it a wasteland, neither pruned nor cultivated,
and briers and thorns will grow there."

Isaiah 5:5-6

At the end of the third day we found ourselves in a vineyard and we took turns getting some shut-eye. One of us was always on the watch for any enemy patrols. We had been lucky so far to keep our canteens filled at the wells we came across as we moved about the area. Food and ammunition were some other concerns. Our boxes of K rations were getting pretty low and our ammunition was not going to hold out much longer.

On the fourth day we could see a company of Germans coming our way–there were at least 200 of them. Tony, Len and I were watching them coming in our direction, down a long ditch that edged the vineyard. They must have seen us in this small vineyard–we were lying down so as not to make too big of a target. When they were within about a hundred yards, we figured that was close enough. We began shooting and we hit a lot of them. We were not in the greatest of positions–lying between the rows of small vines that made up this particular vineyard.

A German machine gun, that was way up on a hill, overlooking the vineyard, kept us pinned down. The guy firing that gun just didn't let up. Then the artillery started to land all around us–they had zeroed in on all of us. The artillery just wouldn't let up until the ground troops got close. We were not letting up either, firing at them and throwing hand grenades. Then the German soldiers who were moving up on us got within hand grenade range. They started to throw them at will.

51

Just the night before in one of our encounters with the Germans, as I mentioned, I got two fingers cut up pretty bad from a bayonet–they were really bothering me. My fingers were now full of dirt and blood, although I had stopped the bleeding, they sure did hurt.

With me in pain and the German machine gun, artillery and hand grenades–we didn't have much luck. On top of everything else that was starting to go wrong, we ran out of ammunition and had no more hand grenades to fling at the Germans. That is the very worst possible situation! We shoved our rifles into the sandy soil of the vineyard and just waited for them.

I had been hit in the back by some shrapnel from the artillery shelling and that pesky machine gunner put six rounds in my rear end. As we were lying there in the vineyard, Tony got a round on top of his head–it put the most perfect part in his short, black hair. Good thing for Tony–the wound wasn't deep–but it sure bled. Len was on my left, quickly grabbing his rear end as he took some rounds there too. My back was sure bleeding bad and my jump jacket, which was really the shirt of our uniform, was partly shot and ripped away.

The three of us just laid there. We could hear the Germans moving up on us. I could hear one of the Germans ask his captain if they should shoot us. When the soldier asked this I figured–this is it. As I said, we were good, we had shot and hurt so many of the German soldiers that mercy was something we were not anticipating. The words of the soldier, "Should we just shoot them?" rang like a bell in my head. Boy did I sweat. I told Tony and Len what the soldier had asked their Captain. The Captain said, "No, these men are wounded so we will take them in." Oh, what sweet relief–was I glad the captain was there to keep us from being shot! A couple of Germans picked me up, took my first aid pack and found the the medication. They opened it and put it in my hand, motioning me to eat it. I made a sign that I needed water and the German captain gave me his own canteen. The

Germans were holding me up because I couldn't stand. I leaned to the right because of the injuries to my back. Then the captain turned to Tony and told him in German to carry me. Tony was dumbfounded–not understanding German, so I told him what the captain had said. Tony tried but the pain almost killed me, so I made him put me down. Two Germans then grabbed me, one on each arm, and I managed to walk up the hill with these two guys helping me. The Germans took all three of us to the ambulance since all three of us were hurt somewhere: Len's rear-end, Tony's head and my back, rear and fingers.

On top of the hill we were loaded into the ambulance–it was a truck, only big enough for the three of us. The trip in the ambulance lasted about a half hour. We had no idea where we were or where we were going. Len's rear was injured, Tony's head was bleeding and my back and rear-end were full of schrapnel or bullets and my fingers were still bleeding. At this point our survival was a result of our training and physical fitness. Now with our injuries, we didn't know what to expect!

# THE FIELD HOSPITAL

The German field hospital consisted of two large tents, one was used for the operating room and the other was where we waited for our turn. The tent where we waited was noisy. Men were lying around on blankets strewn on the dirt floor, moaning and crying out in pain.

At the field hospital we ran into the guy who had the broken leg that we had attended to the first night. His leg still looked like broom-straw. By this time he was completely incoherent and not making any sense at all.

We were escorted into the tent by the German soldiers and we all sat down on blankets–two of us to a blanket. By now it was starting to get dark outside. Into the tent came a German nurse, carrying a hand-powered flashlight. The nurse would pump a small handle on the side of the light and it would generate light. She asked in German who was the worst one. She sounded like she was concerned and told us that the Americans would be the first to be taken care of. I thought to myself, I'm not saying anything–I didn't want them to know I could understand them a little. She repeated this about three times, saying they wanted to help us, "Please, who is the worst one of you?" I finally pointed to the guy with the broken leg. She told the two German medics with her to take him. The medics put him on a stretcher and took him out of the tent. Across the road from our tent was the hospital–every so often we could hear screaming coming from there. I thought, "I don't want to go in there!"

Soon the nurse came back and up to me and asked, "Now who is the worst one?" It is you!" I almost fainted. I told her, "No, just bandage me." So she left and came back with bandages and bandaged all my wounds up.

Laying next to me was an English pilot. I felt real sorry for him because as he lay there the flies were going in and out of his mouth. Every so often I would brush the flies away. Then he started to pull off his watch–he wanted me to have it, but I told him to keep it. He insisted, saying the Germans would just take it anyway. I just put it back on his arm.

The German nurse returned. Coming up to me she again asked who was the worst one. I pointed to the Englishman. She told the two medics to load him up and just then she said, "Halt! Put him back, he's English. Americans first." All the fellas in the tent with me wanted to know what she had said. I told them she had said Americans first. This lifted our morale one hundred percent. We felt a little better after that episode.

For about the next six hours we just laid around the tent. The medics finally brought back the fella with the broken leg. He was patched up with a splint running all the way up to his hip. He was completely oblivious to anything–probably full of ether. When he did wake up he started swearing and cursing the Germans for cutting off his leg. We tried our best to tell him he was luckiest guy in the tent because they had set his leg for him. After he cussed out the German medics for cutting off his leg, we had to take his hand and make him feel his own leg. He was finally satisfied that it was still there. A couple of weeks later we heard a rumor that he was one of the luckiest guys in the invasion–he was successfully repatriated and sent back through the American lines.

The medics continued their work of shuffling guys in and out of the tent. We noticed that they were now bringing German soldiers to the hospital–some of these fellas were wrapped up in parachutes. This did not make us feel very good–those were our chutes.

# ON TO ITALY

During the afternoon three of us, Tony, Len and me, were taken out the hospital tent and placed in a German ambulance for a trip to Italy. This was not how we had envisioned invading the European continent. We were told we were being taken to a small transit camp near Capua, which was supposed to be somewhere near Naples. They drove us to the Straits of Messina where they drove the ambulance right up onto a barge. Before we knew it the barge was underway. We made the trip while riding in the back of the ambulance. The trip took a couple of hours and it was fairly smooth sailing until we sailed into the middle of the war! Looking out the ambulance's window we could see planes fighting one another over the sea. The sky was literally darkened with planes. These pilots were not flying very high since we could hear the noise of their engines and their firing at each other. The noise was just deafening. Occasionally one of the planes would buzz our barge.

The fighter planes above us were dog-fighting each other, but what was worse were the bombs our American planes were dropping–they were trying to hit our barge! Bombs were falling all around us–thank the good Lord, none hit us but some sure came awfully close. We were sure that at any moment we were going to get hit, but luckily we didn't. The bombs were exploding on both sides of our barge. Every now and then one of the fighters, I don't whether they were German or American, would be on fire, with smoke billowing out. We would watch the plane come down and smack the ground or plunge into the water in a thunderous crash.

The Germans would say "the blitz" whenever a P-38 flew over. The P-38 certainly could take command of the sky. It was a twin-fuselage plane and much faster than the German fighter aircraft. From what we could tell the P-38 seemed to have more fire-power too. The Germans were shooting from the ground up. This was difficult to do because the German gunners were firing right into the midst of their own planes that were tangling with the American planes. The Germans were not hitting much, but they sure tried hard. Were we happy when our barge moved out of this area, it was downright dangerous to be out there. When we arrived opposite Messina, over in Italy, the guards took us out of the ambulance and we had to walk a little ways from where the barge landed to the train station.

The streets were filled, and the Italians displayed their anger as soon as they saw us—shaking knives and sickles at us. They hated Americans. We had bombed their cities and homes. It was a good thing the German soldiers were there to protect us from the mob. What an irony!

While we were waiting in the train station we noticed an Italian Army officer walking through the station carrying a small, leather briefcase. One of the German guards asked him what was in the briefcase, so he stopped and opened it. All that was in there was a sandwich and a couple of potatos! We couldn't figure that one out. Where was he going and what was he going to do with only a sandwich and two potatos?

The train finally arrived and we boarded with our guards. It was an extremely slow trip, with a lot of stops along the way. We were told we were headed for Capua, Italy, where a transit prison camp was located. Capua was located about 20 miles due south of Naples, Italy. When we finally arrived in Capua we were again transported via ambulance and taken to the camp. It was somewhere around midnight when we finally got there. After leaving the train I never saw my battling buddies, Tony nor Len, again.

The welcoming committee included several German guards and a German medic. Two of them took me by each arm and helped me from the ambulance. The medic was very nice. As we walked he used a translation book and said, "You are very fortunate, you will be taken care of by an American doctor." Then he asked me if I smoked. I told him I did, but that I didn't have any cigarettes. He pulled out a cigarette and put it in my mouth and lit it. Then he put two more of his cigarettes in my pocket for later. In my mind I thought, "Boy, this man has compassion for another person, regardless of who you were or what uniform you were wearing."

I was taken into the small infirmary. There were only six cots used for beds, the canvas folding type. A Dr. Abrahamson was there to greet us. The fellas carrying me put me down on one of the cots, laying me on my stomach. I couldn't lay on my back due to the injuries. The only light in the room was a small candle in a tin can. Dr. Abrahamson told me the Germans were permitting him to help any wounded Americans that were brought to the camp. The infirmary had been supplied by the Germans with a wash basin, an operating knife or scalpel of sorts, and a small dish of sulfanilamide. It wasn't long before the doctor said, "We'll take care of you now." So I had my shirt and pants removed as I lay there on the cot. The doctor then proceeded to wash my back. There was a soldier assisting the doctor, who the doctor referred to as Red.

When he had finished washing my back, the doctor told Red to bring in the anesthetic. Red said okay and left for a few minutes. He returned shortly with three other guys. The doctor told me to grit my teeth. Each of the fellas grabbed an arm or a leg and held as tight as they could. When the doctor cut into my back it was the worst feeling that could ever happen to a human body. I began to sweat and begged someone to knock me out because the pain was beyond enduring. The doctor continued to sink the knife into my back. I started yelling, "Please, Doc, hit me on the head, knock me out or something!" He just kept on saying, "Grit your teeth". I have never felt such pain before or since then.

The surgery continued as Dr. Abrahamson dug around in the incision with his fingers, trying to find the shrapnel in my back. Each time he found a piece he would say,"Hold on!" Then he would jerk out the piece of metal. After he had removed four pieces, he said he couldn't remove any more because he had no instruments to do so. He assured me that what he had removed should improve my situation considerably. I asked the doctor to save the pieces for me. The metal pieces were the size of quarters. I carried them with me quite a while, but must have lost them somewhere during my imprisonment.

Then the doctor said he would take the bullets out of my buttocks. I begged him not to take them out because my back was giving me so much pain. He agreed to leave them alone for awhile. 'Awhile' has now turned into fifty-nine years. I still carry those six bullets in my rear end. I was completely exhausted by this ordeal.

I was the only patient so I had some peace and quiet in the little hospital. I just laid around the little infirmary for several days while recovering from this surgery. Then one day the door to the infirmary opened and in came a German S.S. officer. He told me to get up and come with him. All I had on was a pair of shorts and a lot of bandages. The guard took me to a building next door to be interrogated by two S.S. officers who each stood about six foot six. On the way out, Dr. Abrahamson, who knew what was coming, told me, "Only give them your name, rank and serial number. Good luck."

I was told to sit down in a straight-back wooden chair in front of a desk. Piled on the desk were papers that other prisoners had apparently filled out. I happened to notice that one document in particular, with a lot of information on it, had been filled out by one of the lieutenants. As curious as I was, I couldn't read it from where I was sitting.

On the other side of the desk was another S.S. officer. First the guy sitting there offered me a cigarette and I told him I didn't smoke. Then he offered me half of his sandwich, and I told him I wasn't very hungry. Really and truly, I would have loved to have taken a cigarette and would have devoured the sandwich; but I thought, "No, it was just their way of softening me up." So the interrogation began.

59

First he asked me where we landed when we jumped. I told him that I didn't know. He asked me what our objective was when we landed. Again I told him I didn't know, and gave him my name, rank and serial number. He told me he already knew that. Next he asked me what General Ridgeway was doing now. I told him that being just a sergeant I had no idea what a General was doing.

Things were not going well. The other guy, who had just been standing there took a black, leather, snake whip down from a hook on the wall. He said, "We have ways of dealing with stubborn sons of bitches like you." He swung the whip across my back so hard I thought he cut me open, the pain was so bad. After he struck me several times I told him that we didn't treat the German prisoners in America like that. I told him they were treated well and fed well, just like our own troops. He stopped and gave me a nasty look while he put the whip back on the hook.

The other guy, still sitting behind the desk, kept asking me questions. What plane was I on? How many planes were there? How many men were in each plane? He even wanted to know where my plane was in the formation? He kept pressing me for our objective on the ground. So I again told him my name, rank and serial number. This brought another outburst. He began swearing at me and again called me a stubborn son of a bitch. He blew smoke from his cigarette in my face, and kept on asking me a lot of questions. Then he told me if I again told him my name, rank and serial number that he would be forced to shoot me for being a spy.

These S.S. officers really knew the good old American slang. They sure could swear. They both seemed to have bad tempers and were mean as heck. Since they were getting no where with me, they took me outside and locked in me a little shed. The shed was a small wooden building, about six feet by five feet. It was full of flies and lice and they almost drove me nuts. There were no windows, just a cot. This cot was filthy and full of lice and fleas. They posted a guard outside the door. The only time he would open the door was to let me out to pee and then it was right back inside. To keep from going crazy I spent the time killing fleas and lice and counted them. Everytime I got to one hundred it seemed I had to pee again. The guard would let me out for that, but put me right back inside. This went on for two days. Finally I complained, "Is this the way you treat wounded soldiers?" At this the guard took me back to the infirmary. Man, did that little infirmary ever look good to me. Doctor Abrahamson went back to work cleaning me up and replacing all the soiled dressings. After a few days of recovering, I felt pretty good again. Of all the prisoners I knew of during the war, not a one had been interrogated as I had.

On Sunday we were told a priest from Rome was coming by to say mass. Anyone who wanted to go was welcome. Several of the prisoners made an altar out of left over packing crates that were just lying around. Some of the German guards even pitched in to help. Being Catholic I asked the doctor if I could go and he said I could if I felt well enough. There was the priest, sporting a full beard. As he started the service a lot of the German guards joined us. At the end, the priest said he would join us again on the following Sunday. He asked how many of us would like a rosary from the Holy Father, Pius XII. Most of us put up our hands indicating we would like to have one. The next Sunday the priest was there and gave each of us a little steel rosary that he said had been blessed by the Holy Father. I carry this rosary to this day.

About a week later I thought my back was finally starting to heal so I told the doctor how good it was feeling and that a scab was forming. Doctor Abrahamson wanted to take a look. As I laid there he grabbed the scab and ripped it off! It felt like a bayonet went into me. I cussed at him and later apologized. He told me he took the scab off because I couldn't have the outside heal before the inside wounds had healed.

61

While my back was slowly healing again, I was having problems with the bullet holes in my buttocks. Not a day went by where I wasn't leaking puss off my rear end. When I got up in the morning my shorts would be stuck to the bullet holes. This continued for over a month. Finally the wounds quit oozing; but the pain never did stop until the mid-1990's. Occasionally I still feel the pain if I sit the wrong way.

# BOXCAR RIDE TO GERMANY

About the time my back was forming another scab we were told to put on our shirt and shoes and go to the waiting trucks. Of course, I wasn't wearing a shirt because of the heavy bandages, so I had to carry my shirt and jump jacket. The trucks took us to the Capua train yard where we were to head north to Germany. While waiting for the trucks where the Germans had us lined up, along came a little German Captain who told the guard to get the men on the trucks faster. The captain told the guard to use his rifle. The guard just stood there, paying no heed to the little Captain. Of course I was standing right in front of this little monster. He grabbed the guard's rifle. As he swung it he smacked me right in the back. This broke open all my incisions and I went down on my knees. Just then I got the rifle butt dead in the middle of my forehead. The stars were flying and I was close to passing out. Two fellas picked me up and I asked them to face me toward the Captain so I could spit in his face. Cooler heads prevailed and they wouldn't let me do it. At this point I really didn't care what happened to me. They said he would have shot me and they were probably right.

We finally got aboard the trucks for our trip to the train yards, where we boarded box cars for the long trip to Germany. Our box cars were of the 40 foot by 8 foot type. We could only guess what had just been in the cars prior to our transport. From all indications they had been loaded with coal because the cars were just filthy. In the middle of the car was one big 25 gallon tin drum to be used as our toilet. It got plenty of use and smelled just awful. The Germans managed to get fifty men into our car. This meant there was not even enough room for all of us to sit down at one time. So half of us sat while the other half stood. This made for a very uncomfortable trip. The train finally pulled out of the yards, carrying us all further from our army and into Nazi-land.

While still in Italy, our train stopped in the Rome depot. There was a man several tracks over from our car. He was a civilian and was watching us and the German soldiers. We noticed him walking very slowly toward us. While he was strolling in our direction he rolled a cigarette. It seemed to us that he was going to talk to us, but there were just too many German soldiers around. So this guy just stopped, winked at us, and kept on walking. Word quickly spread through the car that this guy must be an American spy.

Our car had one small window, about 12 inches by 16 inches. The Germans had covered it with barbed wire to deter anyone from climbing through. Since I could speak German, the fellas in the car would get me up to the window at each stop. I would beg the guards at the stop for drinking water. Here we were in the middle of August and crammed into these hot cars without water. Each time I begged for water the guards would just look at me, spit and walk away. Each and every stop it was the same thing. I would ask in German, "Guard, can we have some drinking water?" They would just look up, no feeling or emotion displayed, and spit, and walk away.

At this time all I had for clothing was a pair of pants and shoes. I was for the most part covered with bandages. The bandages by now were just black from all the coal dust in the car. On the fifth day out, the train stopped in some little town. While I was up at the window I could see a water pump a little ways off in the distance. I went through my usual routine of calling to the guard for water. To my shock and surprise, there was the kind German medic I had met in Capua. When he saw me he asked me what I was doing in there. He said I belonged in the car with the wounded. I told him that I had nothing to say about it, but was just put in the car. He immediately told the guard to open the door and told me to come out. I told him that none of us in the car had any water to drink in five days. He took me to the pump and told me to wash my hands and face. I drank and drank. Then he

65

got several buckets and we filled them and passed them up to the fellas in my box car. We kept this up until everyone had their fill.

Then I was led up the train to another box car where the wounded were sitting on straw strewn around on the car's floor. We were all Americans, but I didn't know any of these other wounded men. Relatively speaking, my back was somewhat improved by now. I rode for two more days in that car before we came to Stalag 2B. Our trip by train from Capua to Stalag 2B had taken us seven days. Some of the Germans told us that this stalag was in Prussia, way up in northern Germany.

# STALAG 2B
## (Early August 1943 - October 1943)

Welcome to the Stalag. Stalag comes from a contraction of two words: *stamm* and *lager*, meaning, main camp. Stalags were used to hold enlisted men who were prisoners of war. Stalag 2B was located just west of Hammerstein in what was referred to as old Prussia. It was about 100 miles southwest of Gdansk, Poland, or Danzig. If it would have been anything like *Hogan's Heros* I would wish I was still there.

The Germans must have had some pretty good intelligence. They seemed to have a special respect for paratroopers. In their General Orders pertaining to prisoners of war, number 576 it says, "...paratroopers are to be assigned to work in closed groups and under special guard."[4] We were soon to discover what all that was about.

Rumors run fast and wild in the Army, and prisoners of war were no exception. We had heard that this was considered to be the worst stalag in all of Germany because of the mean staff of guards. Upon our arrival we were unloaded from the train at the camp and immediately counted. They counted us three times before they were satisfied we were all there. We were then led into the barracks where we all had our own bunk. It was made of wood, like shelves or bunk beds. There were no mattresses, only about an inch of straw for padding. We were all whistled out of the barracks eight to ten times a day and made to stand in lines, behind one another, just to be counted.

---

4    *German Orders*, Supreme Command of the Wehrmacht, (Berlin-Schoeneber, 16 June 1941), page 10 of 20. Orders located by a member of the Provost Marshal General's Office shortly after the conclusion of hostilities, translated by General B.M. Bryan's office.

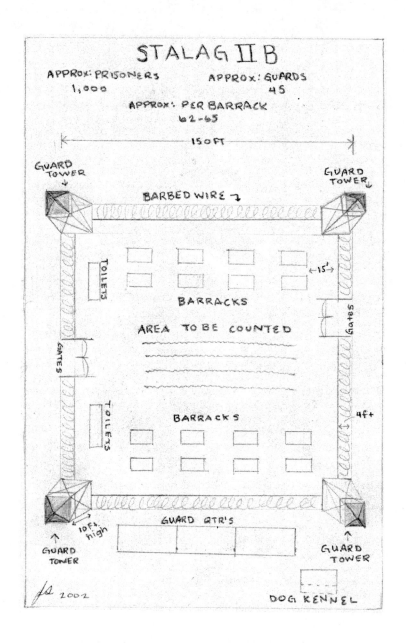

# STALAG II B

APPROX: PRISONERS
1,000

APPROX: GUARDS
45

APPROX: PER BARRACK
62-65

150 FT

GUARD TOWER

GUARD TOWER

BARBED WIRE

TOILETS

BARRACKS

15'

Gates

AREA TO BE COUNTED

Gates

TOILETS

BARRACKS

4 ft

10 Ft. high

GUARD TOWER

GUARD QTR'S

GUARD TOWER

JS 2002

DOG KENNEL

68

We didn't get much food. Each day we were given one slice of bread and one cup of soup, which was mostly just warm water.

We lost some of our buddies to the cold and some to the sicknesses that were rampant in the camp. During the cold Autumn, if someone died, he was held up to be counted for his slice of bread. There were several occasions when there was more than one dead man being held up just to be counted for his slice of bread. We would hold these men up back in the third row so they would not be noticed. It seems we would do almost anything for food. After the Germans discovered the dead soldiers they would take them out of the camp. We never found out what they did with these soldier's bodies.

The camp was about the size of two football fields sitting parallel to each other. There were two barbed wire fences, the interior and the exterior, each about ten feet high. The area between the fences was about four feet, which the Germans had filled with concertina wire. At each corner of the camp was a wooden guard tower, the floor of the tower was about level with the ten foot high fence. Inside our camp were sixteen wooden barracks buildings. Each of the buildings housed about 48 men, twelve double bunk beds to each wall. There were five bare light bulbs hanging from the ceiling of each barrack. We also had some light during the day from the six windows in the walls. The narrow end of each building had a door. In the center of the camp, between the two gates was the area in which we were incessantly counted. From what we could tell, there seemed to be about 45 very mean German men assigned to this camp, with dogs of similar disposition.

There were no showers at Stalag 2B during my stay. About once a week we were permitted to wash our clothes in a bucket. The Germans only turned on the water at certain times. We also had a bucket for drinking water.

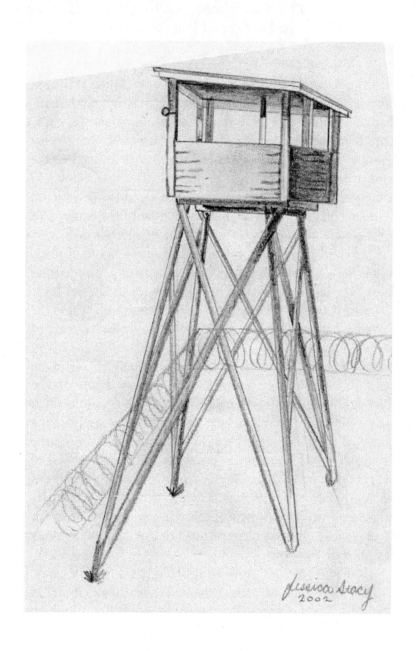

One of the first orders of business after we arrived at the Stalag was to be issued our German "dog tags." They were made out of lightweight metal, about two inches by three inches, with a perforation in the middle. On each side of the perforation your name and German prisoner of war identification number was printed. We all wore these around our necks on a piece of string. I can still remember my number to this day–20623.

Occasionally we would volunteer for work details out of the camp just to get away for a day. They had us cleaning the streets of Hammerstein of debris after the American and British bombers went through. We recognized that the area was not a primary target. The bombers were usually headed back to England, but always seemed to have a couple of bombs left for their return trip.

We had a big old German sergeant for a guard at Stalag 2B who we called Pistol Pete. Pete was originally from Pittsburg, Pennsylvania and one of our guys recognized him. He was scared to death and did not want Pete to see him. When we were called out to be counted he would always stand in back in the third row. Old Pete would get up in front of us and pull out his pistol and say to us, "Don't any of you sons of bitches try to escape, cause I have many notches on my pistol for those who have tried before and never made it." Our guy said he remembered Pete from back in the States and said he lived a couple of blocks from him. He said Pete was always mean to the kids and they were all frightened by him. Old Pete had a bad habit of calling us out at all hours of the day and night to be counted. He didn't trust us for fear we would try to escape.

One night about twelve guys tried to escape by jumping off the roof and over the fence, but someone must have leaked word out, because when they jumped the machine guns killed all of them before they hit the ground. No one ever found out who leaked the information. From then on we were mustered out more than ever to be counted. They would

71

count one way and then count the other way, no trust in this bunch. The Germans always had their dogs with them, big German shepherds–and boy, were they mean. When they blew the whistle we found we had better make tracks to get lined up before they started counting. On many occasions we had several fellas sick who couldn't get up. The Germans never checked, they simply sent the dogs in to help them get out of bed. The Germans allowed the dogs to bite and chew on your arms and legs before they called them off.

The treatment at Stalag 2B was just terrible. I hate to disagree with Military Intelligence Service of the War Department, but their report of July 15, 1944 on Stalag 2B did not reflect the conditions of the camp during August to October of 1943. The official report from 1944 said that the major portion of the prisoners' food came from Red Cross parcels. Well, I am here to tell you that we didn't see any Red Cross parcels. We saw lots of guards and German officers smoking American cigarettes, so we had a pretty good idea who received those Red Cross parcels. If I had been fed decent meals I would not have gone from 180 pounds to 113 pounds in twenty-one months. The official report got one thing right, it said, "Treatment was worse at Stalag 2B than at any other camp in Germany established for American PW's before the Battle of the Bulge. Harshness at the base stalag degenerated into brutality and outright murder on some of the kommandos.[5] Beatings of Americans on kommandos by the German overseers were too numerous to list."[6] But, with the hope of better conditions, small groups of prisoners would

---

5    A Kommando was a work-crew of about twenty prisoners who were housed away from the Stalag. In my case we were housed at a farm in the vicinity of the Stalag.

6    *Stalag 2B*, American Prisoners of War in Germany, (Prepared by Military Intelligence Service, War Department, 15 July 1944), page 3 of 6.

volunteer to be taken out of the stalag for work. They would live in different places such as farms or along railroad tracks. So after several months in the camp, a group of us volunteered to go out on a kommando. Kommandos were what the Germans called the work details for the prisoners. We all thought that we would get better food and treatment if we worked. It didn't happen. They worked us from daylight 'til dark everyday.

# SCHULENBERG KOMMANDO
## (October 1943 until January 1945)

There were twenty-two of us in my group and we were sent to a place called Schulenberg approximately 35 miles away. We walked all the way. This was typical of the work kommandos that prisoners of war volunteered for. Most kommandos consisted of about 30 men doing farm labor.[7] Schulenberg was a large family farm, named for the owners, the Schulenberg's. It was near a little village called Flattie, about thirty miles from a town called Deutschkrone When we arrived we were put in a barn that had originally been a hog barn–yes, a pig-sty. The inside had two long beds running from one wall to the other on each side of the barn. Half of us were on one side and half on the other. This barn had two electric lights in the ceiling, the kind with one bulb and a pull string. There were only enough blankets for half of us, one blanket for two men.

That first night we were exhausted from the long march and we all hit the sack early since there weren't enough blankets for all of us, so we each had to share one–imagine, two grown men to one small Army blanket. During the night we could feel something crawling all over us and I asked the fella next to me, "Do you feel something?" Just about then someone in the barn shouted, "Rats!" We all shook our blankets and you could hear the rats hitting the floor and scurrying away. This was about all for sleeping that night.

---

7    *Camp Conditions - General*, American Prisoners of War in Germany, (Prepared by Military Intelligence Service, War Department, 15 July 1944), page 2 of 4.

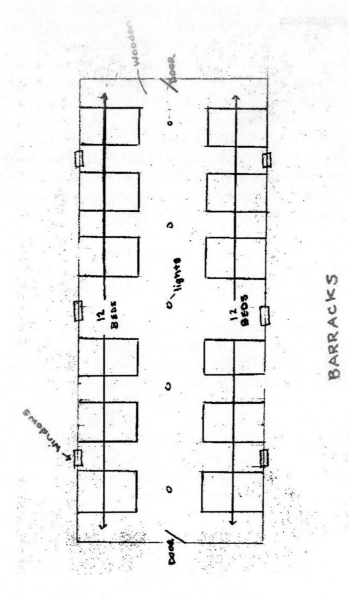

BARRACKS

For the next four nights we fought with the rats, before we finally won and got rid of the rats. However, "When the rats are away the mice will play." Yes, next there were mice. There wasn't any way we could win until one day, while out working, we captured a young weasel. We brought him back and made a cage for him. He was one contented weasel–we kept him full of mice. Soon our problem with mice was over. We kept this little weasel out of sight from the guards and just kept feeding him mice every day.

In time the conditions improved somewhat in our pig-sty. The local carpenter, Mr. Koplein, installed bunks and two long wooden tables with a bench for each side of the tables. The building had one small, square, wood-burning stove, but it was rare that we had any wood to burn.

There were four Russian prisoners at this farm, but the Germans kept them separated from us. One day though, one of the Russians named Mike called over to us and said he had caught a large rat. He wanted to know if we wanted to put him in with our weasel. We figured, why not, and gave it a try. The cage we had built had two compartments, so we had the weasel on one side and the rat on the other. Then we opened the door and the weasel went over to the rat's side. When that weasel saw the rat it started running around in circles. It was moving so fast we wondered if it would get dizzy. When the weasel finally stopped moving the rat grabbed him. We all got excited, thinking the rat would kill our weasel, so the guys pulled open the cage and tried to stomp on the rat. These animals were not just going to sit there, they made a bee-line for the barn doors. Now there were two small openings in the bottom of the door and they both squeezed through.

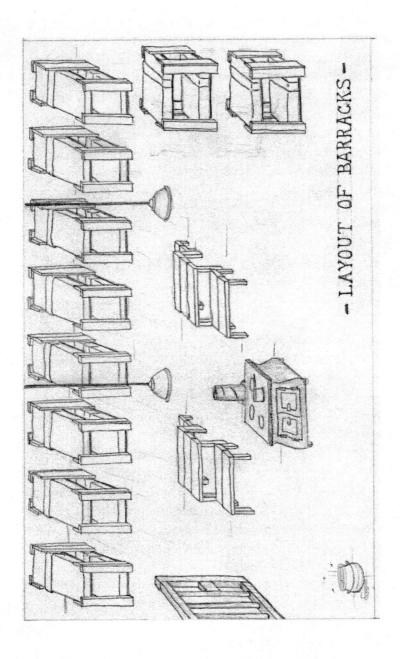

- LAYOUT OF BARRACKS -

Next morning, as the guards got us out and lined up for counting, the lady from the big farm house came by. She stopped and talked to the guards and I overheard her say that she found about a dozen baby turkeys dead. She said there must be a weasel around here that is killing her baby turkeys. Of course, every time the Germans would talk, the fellas all asked me what they were saying. I told them don't mention the word weasel or we may be shot. I filled them in on what our weasel was suspected of doing. This continued for several days, same story every time. The lady would go out to the hen house in the morning and find numerous dead baby turkeys. Needless to say, we were all very careful about not mentioning our weasel.

Everyone from the dorf and those who lived at Schulenberg's Farm worked for the Schulenbergs. Most of the hands worked the fields, some took care of the cattle, one was a blacksmith and one was the cabinet-maker, Mr. Koplein, a very skilled craftsman.

Once a month I was selected to go with Mr. Koplein into the forest to mark trees for cutting. Every time I went with him he brought me a sandwich. It consisted of two large pieces of dark bread smothered in goose fat. Let me tell you, it tasted better than cake. I really looked forward to this day of going out and marking trees...and to that wonderful lunch. No guard was with us, but Mr. Koplein did have a gun. I doubt he would have used it on me. Mr. Koplein was one terrific carpenter. He also was the farm's snuff-maker. Every morning the men from the dorf would come by for their daily supply. They would stop by his shop and load up on snuff every day. These old German men didn't put it in their lip like most snuff users, they sniffed it right up their nose.

Schulenberg Farm

In the morning the cows were milked and in late morning the milk truck would come by for the pickup. This milk truck was powered by a wood-burning engine with a large tank behind the cab. The gas given off from the burning wood went through a filter and propelled the engine. It seemed as though it was awfully powerful for just burning wood. As we watched, the driver would occasionally stop and put a sack of wood-chips in the top of the burner.

The blacksmith it seemed could make or repair just about anything mechanical. He was certainly clever. The wheels on the farm's wagons were not far enough apart to avoid crushing a row of potatoes as it was drawn through the field. He realized that just by taking the wheel off and turning it around, mounting it backwards, there would be enough clearance for the wagon's wheels to travel between the rows.

Every now and then during the summer, a guard would come in on a Saturday and tell us we were going to the Bahnhoff, or train depot. There would be three or four box-cars full of fertilizer. This bulk fertilizer looked like salt and tasted like it too. This stuff was four feet high and the interior of the boxcar was full. We would shovel the fertilizer into wagons and the German hired-hands would haul the wagons back to Schulenberg's.

It was the summer of 1944 and was it hot! We were all sweating so bad and we were covered from head to toe with this salty fertilizer. One day while we were unloading the stuff the head guard came over to me and said, "Edward, when we get through unloading this fertilizer and if all the men behave, we will all go into the depot and have a glass of cold beer." When I told the fellas the good news, they were so elated that they almost buried me in fertilizer. True to his word, when we were finished, we all went inside the station and had a stein of beer. We thought we had died and gone to heaven. It certainly tasted out of this world and it was a gesture of kindness I will never forget. It was about the only nice thing these guards ever did for us.

In our barracks back at the farm we had a little stove but the Germans would not give us any wood or coal to keep warm with in the winter. Throughout the winter we all had to scrounge for pieces of wood or steal wood any way that we could just to keep from freezing. It was always cold in our barracks during the winter months since we only had a fire once in awhile.

Surviving was a priority. We did not have a lot of clothing and what we had was generally in pretty bad shape. I had my jump jacket, but the back had been badly ripped up back in the vineyard. Under that I had a shirt. I had a pair of pants and my boots. Boots without socks provide little warmth. Most of the fellas would sit around with our German issue blankets. These were wool, brownish-gray in color. Our bunks at Schulenberg were two-levels, of wooden boards, about three by six feet.

One of our guys at Schulenberg was Johnny. Johnny was from the south and he would ask what time it was at least ten times every day. Then we learned that Johnny never went beyond the second grade and had not learned to tell time.

Once a month we were given post-cards and told to write a note home to our families and tell them we were alive and well. Most of us figured that the cards were probably thrown away, but some got through. It all depended on what kind of mood the guards were in. The cards might be mailed or tossed in the trash. A couple of mine actually did get through to my dad back in St. Paul. We were told we could only write what was on the board. As I recall, the wording they provided was something like, "I am well and being treated fine. I hope to be home soon."

We noticed that Johnny never took the time to write and he would generally give his card away. I told him that his mom, or the girlfriend he always spoke of marrying after the war, would surely want to hear from him and know that he was okay. I wrote a sample for Johnnyy, but he just couldn't do it. So I would write his card for him, telling his mom that he was well and I certainly hope she got the cards. I'm not sure she was aware that Johnny couldn't read or write, but we wrote and sent the cards anyway.

There were several of us who spent a lot of time with Johnny teaching him to tell time and to write. To help Johnny tell time, we drew pictures of a clock on a piece of paper and would quiz him about the time as we changed the placement of the clock hands. Telling time was the easy part, we spent hours teaching Johnny to write. This took about nine or ten months and had to be done in the evening after our work was done. We didn't have much time for teaching. At one point Johnny said he didn't want to learn. We suggested that if he got home and married his girl, she might give him a grocery list and ask him to run to the store and pick up a few items. Would he walk into the store and hand the slip to the cashier and say I need these items? "Could you get them for me because I can't read or write?" Basically we embarrassed Johnny into learning. He thought about what we said and agreed that it was best to learn. After that it was study every night. We were all pleased by the progress Johnny was making. He was finally able to print words.

During the summer and fall we worked in the potato fields each day from sun-up 'til sun-down. In the potato fields the men from the farm would drive the horses that pulled the potato machine. Schulenberg's had five potato harvesting machines. Each machine was pulled by three horses. At the front of the potato digger was a blade that dug up the potatoes with a paddle-wheel just to the rear. This paddle would throw the potatoes into the field for the rest of us to pick up. The faster the horses were driven, the faster the machine dug up the taters, and the further the paddles would throw them. Generally the potatoes were thrown in a patch spreading ten to twelve feet across. Each of us had a space to glean the thrown potatoes from. We would gather the potatoes and put them in wooden half-barrels. Two of our guys would then come along with a wagon and we would have to hoist these half-barrels and dump them in the wagon. This work kept us jumping. We had to pick up all our potatoes before the next machine would come by and throw more. All day long you were bending over.

The twenty-one of us prisoners were on one side of a field picking potatoes, under the watchful eyes of six armed German soldiers; and, on the other side of the field, about 250 feet away, were the women and children from the farm. They too were picking potatoes as the potato machines threw them. One of the ladies who was picking potatoes with us looked shockingly like my mom who had been dead about eleven years. This was an eery reminder of her. Finally, when we were apparently done picking up potatoes, the guards would line us up on one end of the field and have us walk the field one last time to pick up any little potatoes we may have missed. Not to be thought of as kind or gentle-hearted, when the potatoes were cleaned out of the field, the guards would have us go back over the field and remove any rocks to a large pile.

The next step was running the potatoes through a potato machine that sorted them by size. After sorting them we put them in trenches about four feet deep, covered them with straw, and put about a foot of dirt on top of them to keep them from freezing in the winter. This is how we stored them until they were needed. This digging trenches and burying potatoes was back-breaking work!

After the potato work was done they kept us busy with other jobs. Working in the fuel manufacturing plant was one way the Germans kept us busy after the potato harvest. Things could not get started at the plant until the potatoes and beets had been harvested. The Germans somehow used this salad concoction for fuel in their fighter planes. The potatoes and beets were dumped into a large distillery and mixed to produce fuel.

Potato Picking

The guards provided us with 55 gallon drums to fill with this fuel. While we were filling these drums from the distilled vegetables a German officer would be sitting and watching our every move. As we finished filling each drum, we would funnel off a small sample and give it to the officer who would go somewhere with it, presumably for sampling its effectiveness.

The hard work came after we filled these barrels. With three of us pushing and two of us pulling on ropes we had fastened on each end of the barrel, we would struggle to get the drum out of the basement of the distillery where we had filled them. Each time we got this assignment we would fill somewhere between twenty-five to thirty barrels. This assignment came our way twice a week for about two months each fall.

Every evening the guards would take away our shoes and pants before locking us up for the night. On one particular morning when they unlocked the door and threw our shoes and pants in, one of our guys named Tim, couldn't find his shoes. When he told the guard, the German produced a pair of wooden shoes and told him to put them on. Tim said he couldn't walk in them and he wasn't going to wear them. The guard became infuriated and stuck Tim in the face with his bayonet! It went in his cheek and came out near one of his eyes. The blood squirted all over the place as Tim dropped to the ground. The Germans took him away and we never saw him again.

While at Schulenberg I came down with dysentery. It was so bad it seemed to last forever–32 days. This was during the fall potato harvest and every time I so much as bent over a little I had to run and...you know what. This was just awful, no toilet paper and no leaves on the trees. I picked up every scrap of paper I could find and saved them. There's a tree in the area of Schulenberg that must be 900 feet high or at least the tallest in Germany, because that tree got more fertilizer as the unloading point for dysentery. It really took its toll on me.

85

You can't imagine how sore my bottom was. Without toilet paper I just used all those scraps of paper I picked up along the road for such emergencies. After about two weeks of this the guards thought I was going to die (I should have been so lucky!). They gave me a small charcoal-like pill and a cup of tea to wash it down. This remedy sort of helped. At least I was able to keep on working. Finally after 32 days it stopped. But just my luck, about two months later I got it again. After the first couple of days there is nothing left to come out but green foam. I had to put up with a sore rear end all over again.

One of the fellas in camp was Artie, from New York. We called him "Russ" because he was of Russian descent. He never came down with dysentery, but the guards knew Artie was regular. Every morning at 5 AM Artie was up and pacing the floor. He would be saying, "Where are those s.o.b.s?" He would pace and repeat this over and over until we heard the iron bars on the door drop. It got so that when the guards dropped that last iron bar, they would just step back because Artie was on his way out like a bull. One morning Artie was heading for the throne and on his way he was pulling down his pants. Just as he got there and sat down a huge rat, the size of a cat, jumped up in his lap. Needless to say, Artie came out of there yelling–he and the rat heading in different directions. From that day forward, Artie always made a lot of noise on his way to the throne–hopefully to scare off any rats that were hanging around.

Every couple of weeks, on a Saturday morning, the head guard would come and say, "I need two men for toilet cleaning." He always said this in German. Two men had to go and get one of the farm's horses, put on the harness, and head for the toilets.

There were about twenty-two of us at Schulenberg so we could alternate the toilet detail. The toilets were three steps up and the doors to the waste box were on the side. After opening the doors we would hook onto two rings on the box beneath the seats. The horse pulled the box out and off we headed to the manure pile. You drove the horse to the pile and emptied the box by turning it over and then sweeping it out with a shovel. We were constantly being warned not to make the pile wider, just higher. Then you had the horse haul the box back to the toilet and you pushed the box back in place. There were about ten toilets in the camp. We called this duty the *honey-dumper job*. There was no cleaning up after this detail, cleanliness was no better at Schulenberg than at Stalag 2B.

One day the camp overseer asked me if I had any relatives in the Reich. I told him that I had family in Illmitz, Austria. He asked me if I wanted him to write to them and let them know that I was in Germany. This sounded like a pretty good idea to me. So he wrote to my family: grandparents on my mom's side, some aunts and uncles, and lots of cousins. It wasn't long before we got a letter in return–the relatives said they were going to come and see me. Well, the overseer wrote back as soon as he could, warning them not to come. He feared that upon their arrival we all may have been shot. In their letter I learned that my grandfather had passed away just a short time before. As a prisoner of war in Germany, I knew about my grandfather's death two years before my dad and family. I delivered the news when I returned home in the summer of 1945.

At the Schulenberg lock-up we had a fence outside our door. It was a barbed-wire fence, about ten feet high. The wire was so thick and tight you could hardly get your hand through it. On Saturdays we would be let out in the little yard, about five feet by fifteen feet, to wash our clothes. All this amounted to was rinsing them out in some water, no one had any soap, and very little clothes. We didn't want to wear them out washing them.

I still had my safety razor at this point, but there were about fifteen of us using the same blade for over a year. We kept trying to maintain its sharpness by rubbing the double-edge razor blade on broken bottles. We just used our imagination–telling ourselves it was sharp. It really didn't make any difference, we all used it anyway. On this particular Saturday, a young boy, maybe 14 or 15 years old, came walking by and greeted us. We all said hello. I noticed that he had a barber comb and a straight razor in his shirt pocket. I asked him where he was going and he told us he was heading to Flattie, which was the next village from our camp. He said he was going to school there, learning to be a barber. I asked him if he would like to practice on us–no one else was cutting our hair or shaving us. He said he would like that, so we told him to ask the head guard if he could come in and practice on us. The head guard said it was okay since we were beginning to look pretty shabby. So the kid came back that afternoon and stopped by. The guards unlocked the gate and the kid came in and started cutting hair. He cut for a couple of hours before he told us he had to go. He said he would be back the next week. When he left I heard him telling the guards that he would be back the following week to cut more hair. Before the kid left, we asked him if he really needed his straight razor, whether he could get another one. He said getting another would be no problem and thus we got ourselves a razor that actually cut.

One day I came down with a terrible toothache. I told the guard that I needed to see a dentist. He told me that he would check on it. The head guard told one of the soldiers, named Rotsicka, to take me into town to see the dentist. There was only one dentist in our area, in a town about thirteen miles away. We marched all the way down this concrete highway, just me and the guard. Surprisingly, not one car or truck passed us all day, going or coming. When we arrived, the guard told the dentist to be careful, that I could understand and speak German. Sitting alone in the waiting area, the guard left the dentist and me in private. The doctor told me he had relations in Chicago and I said, "You do? Well I might just know them! I live very close to Chicago." Well, he and I were friends right away. Since there was no electricity he had a girl who would pump for the drill to work. He cleaned up the tooth and filled the cavity. He told me it was a temporary filling and to come back the next week for the final filling because he wanted to talk more with me. As we were leaving, no further than a few steps from his office, I spit, and there went the new filling. So I had to make that thirteen mile hike again the next week. I didn't mind, it got me away from the camp, and the dentist and I could talk. He would go on about his relatives in Chicago and I told him I would look them up when I got home–if I ever got home.

Occasionally we would be promised Red Cross parcels. These had food and cigarettes in them. We really looked forward to getting these. The day they were to arrive the guards would tell us the train got bombed by our air force so there wouldn't be any parcels. One day our camp had a visit from a German Colonel. Normally the highest ranking German in camp was a captain. Let me tell you, those guards were all at attention! When the colonel came into our barracks I noticed he was smoking an American cigarette. I asked him where he got it and he told me some American gave it to him. We didn't buy that for a minute. He got that cigarette out of the Red Cross packages that were meant for us. Contrary to what Military Intelligence said, we never saw any Red Cross packages.[8]

We had some guards at Schulenberg that were downright mean. It was nothing to get hit with the butt of a

---

8      Military Intelligence Service, War Department, *Stalag 2B*, (American Prisoners of War in Germany, 15 July 1944), 1. This report stated that a "major portion of POWs' food comes from weekly Red Cross parcels."

rifle for the most insignificant things, such as breaking a shovel or pick handle. All this abuse was uncalled for, but I guess the Germans had to take their hatred out somewhere and we prisoners were handy.

During the Spring of 1944, Al and Jim, a couple of G.I.s decided to escape. We all talked about it for a couple of days before their attempt. One day when we came in from working the fields they were gone. The Germans were not pleased, so they locked us all up for about a week in the pigsty and would not open the door for any reason. We never found out what happened to Al or Jim, whether they made it or not.

On a sunny Saturday afternoon, when all was quiet, the sky turned black by hundreds of our bombers going over. The air raid sirens were blowing and the bombers looked like they were on a joy ride. As soon as the sirens began blowing everyone in the camp took off running for shelter. Everyone except us of course. There was nowhere for us to run–we were just lucky enough not to have been hit. Soon, off in the distance, we could hear the bombs exploding as they hit the ground. We often wished they would just save one bomb for us–to sort of end it all real quick. Not far from the camp there was a battery of anti-aircraft guns. They would only shoot after the planes were past. One day after this happened, the planes must have saved one bomb for the gun. On the return trip a plane dropped a bomb and from then on everything was quiet. The gun remained silent from then on whenever the bombers flew over. Evidently the gun must have infuriated someone on one of those bombers, so he probably figured he had better take care of that gun before he got hurt.

After we had completed most of the farm work we were sent to work on the railroad. We tamped ties, changed rail, and tightened bolts at the rail joints. Every so often we would break off a bolt at the rail joint–our little bit of sabotage. Lifting rail was not easy. We usually got about twenty men involved in lifting and carrying the rail. The German overseer would get mad and complain that it only took nine Russian girls to lift and carry a rail. We told him we weren't used to that kind of work.

The head supervisor of the detail, Louie, obviously trying to learn English, was always asking us a lot of questions. "What do we call a hammer?" What do we call a wrench?" What do we call a shovel?" We always made up some nasty name figuring he would never know the difference. One day when the supervisor was down on his hands and knees lining up some track, he asked what we called the track. Everyone had a different answer for him. We decided on "Kiss my a__." Here was this supervisor, down on all fours, lining up the track, shouting, "Kiss my a__." You know, before long we got kind of used to hearing him shout that out and no longer paid much attention. This supervisor also wanted to know what *son of a bit__* meant. We simply told him it was slang for releasing tension. We were hoping no German who knew English would come by and hear the words we had taught the rail supervisor for the various tools.

One day this supervisor asked me to check with my comrades and find out who could operate a bulldozer. I thought, none of the guys are going to get that job, I would take it. I told him I could operate one and he thought that was just wonderful. He said a guy named Herman would take me over to the shed and show me the machine. So as we headed over to the shed, I got to thinking, "I don't know a darn thing about a bulldozer." What would I tell him when we got there? Once inside the shed I walked up to the bulldozer and looked it over real good, like I knew what I was looking at. I said, "You know, Herman, it's a little different than the ones we have in America." Herman replied, "I should think so."

So Herman showed me how to start it on benzine, then to switch it over to diesel. We climbed aboard and he showed me the pedals and levers. Boy, after getting all the instructions I felt like a bulldozer operator. I couldn't wait to get started. The next day I got my first baptism of operating a bulldozer. We hooked onto a machine and headed out along the railroad tracks. When the fellas saw me they all wanted to know when it was their turn on the machine. I just told them it wasn't a kids toy, that it was serious business and took a skilled operator.

Everything seemed to be going along fine. With the bulldozer I was pulling a machine that dug up the dirt with a fan-like wheel and then threw the dirt along the railroad right of way. All of sudden, the man riding on the machine went flying through the air, right by me. I stopped immediately and jumped down. When I picked him up he said we had hit a large stone with the mechanism that resulted in breaking the machine. He told me we would have to take the machine to the local blacksmith for repairs. They had another digging machine, so we used the replacement to continue working. Our work went on for several weeks, grading the railroad right of way. This all had to be done to exchange the broken rail with usable second hand rail.

Our work had taken us about 40 miles from our barracks so we had to wait for the train to return to pick us up. Some days the train was late so we just sat and waited for it to arrive. When it reached us we would all get in our private car, a box car with a big sign on the side, "Prisoners of War." It was usually dark when we got back to our barracks, so we were ushered in and locked up immediately.

# DETTEMENN DORF-KELSO
## (January 1945 to May 1945)
How horrible it all was!

Many have heard of the Bataan Death March. There was another death march, one conducted by the Germans during the dead of winter.[9]

One bitter, cold morning in January of 1945, we were rousted out and told we were leaving. The weather was like I was used to back home in Minnesota, lots of snow and very cold. We started marching and would keep moving until we came to a barn big enough to house us all for the night. There were about 100 prisoners in this march. It was about 20° below zero and most of us didn't have any socks to wear, just bare feet inside our boots that were like a couple of boards. At night in the barns we would take our boots off and pour the blood out. It seemed like we each had about a shot-glass full of blood in our boots from the walking. We would shove our feet into piles of straw, hoping for a little warmth, but there was none to be found. In the morning we had to put our boots back on—it wasn't easy over raw feet. It was just hell walking the first mile or two, but the farther we went, it all just settled down into a painful march. One time we noticed one of our guards take off his boots and for socks he only had rags wrapped around his feet. We figured things were not going too well for Germany if even their soldiers had no socks. From our perspective though, rags were at least better than nothing.

---

9     For additional information, refer to: Gary Turbak, *Death March Across Germany*, published in VFW magazine and on-line at, www.b24.net/pow/march.htm

1,000 Mile March

We would generally cover about 25 to 30 miles a day. Sometimes the snow was up to our knees. We just kept going. With a guy next to you prodding you with his rifle and bayonet, there was nothing else to do but take the next step. This march that had started the second week of January, continued until the last week of February 1945. We figured we probably walked about 1,000 miles. We kept going in a generally south-western direction, toward the American lines, because the Germans did not want us to fall into the hands of the Russians.

We lost a lot of men on the march. Some of the fellas died in the wagons and sometimes they would just fall out to the side of the road. When that happened, a guard would stay with them and then later the guard would come running up to the group alone.

Somewhere south of Berlin, before we started heading northwest, we were marching through some small town and there was a fella standing there in civilian clothes, just watching us. As we went by he winked and said in a low tone, "Keep your chins up, it won't be long now." We figured he must have been one of our intelligence agents.

During this stint we weren't fed much. Each day we got one slice of bread and one boiled potato. The inside of my mouth became all blistered. Even though I was hungry, I couldn't drink water or eat my bread or potato. I just gave it away. This went on for five days. I thought I was going to die of starvation, not being able to eat. I was later told that this was a symptom of malnutrition or starvation.

While we were on the march, one of the guys named Simms, got such frozen feet that he couldn't get his shoes on. The Germans gave him a pair of straw shoes, these looked like a pair of overshoes. He put these on and the Germans allowed him to ride in their equipment wagon. None of us escaped the problem. Eventually, all of us ended up with frost-bitten feet. This was sure getting to be old, marching day in and day out in knee-deep snow and without socks. If only the weather could have been warmer.

Eventually we got to a little hamlet called Dettemenn Dorf-Kelso, just west of the city of Rostock. We were housed on the second floor of a building. Our barracks consisted of a number of bunk beds lining two walls with one table and two benches in the center of the room. Just off our room was another smaller room, sort of a closet. Here the guards would lock up our clothes at night to discourage our trying to escape. All we were left to sleep in were our green boxer shorts. Outside, down a wooden walk-way, was our toilet.

Every morning before going to work, repairing the railroad by changing damaged rails or tamping ties, there was a chore for two men to empty the toilet can. The can was kept in our barracks and we used it throughout the night. We would empty it in the outhouse behind our barracks. One morning as Cliff and I entered the long outhouse we saw a chicken inside. I said, "Don't let him get away. As soon as you get him, twist his neck and put him in the can." We approached him very carefully and I got him by the neck. One quick twist and he never made a sound. Into the can he went and we covered him up with the lid. That evening in our potato soup we had chicken. It was impossible for us to see the chicken, but we knew it was in there. Another night, our cook, South Carolina Jim, told us he had a treat for us in our soup. After we were through eating, we asked him, "What was the treat?" Our soup was always so watery it was difficult to tell if anything was in it. He told us he had caught a cat and cooked it in the soup. None of us could tell what it was, it didn't hurt anyone, and besides, it tasted pretty good.

About an hour after eating, around 7:30 in the evening, Henry the guard would open the door and just stand there. He had come to take us for our drinking water. We had to walk to the train depot to pump our water. We hauled the water in a 25 gallon can which two of us would carry. On the way I would ask Henry how the war was going. He would tell me just where the American and Russian fronts were. Our

97

conversations went on like this every night. Henry kept us up to date on the progress the allies were making.

One night about 9:00 PM we heard the movement of the iron bar that locked our door. In walked Henry. He had always treated us well besides keeping us up to date on the war's progress. He called for me and told me to sit down. I sat down on a bench at this little table across from Henry and he pulled out his wallet. He removed some pictures and handed them to me. The first was a picture of a beautiful woman, his wife. Then there was a picture of his two children, they were about 10 or 12 years old. Finally, there was a picture of his home. He looked at me and just started to cry, saying, "That was yesterday, today I have nothing." He kept repeating this over and over, "Today I have nothing." Evidently, our bombers came over and hit his house with his wife and children inside. He said there was nothing left. His family and home were in Aachen. The tears rolled down his face as he cried. I felt so bad for him that I too cried with Henry as did all the rest of us. All I could say was how horrible it all was. The war was destroying everything. He told me that he didn't blame the pilots because they had a job to do just like we have. Henry was the nicest German guard we ever had. That made two Germans that were decent to us, Henry and the German medic.

# THE RUSSIANS ARE COMING

One night while laying in my bunk I thought I could see flashes of light through the barred window. I looked for a while and then I saw more flashes and pretty soon I could hear muffled explosions off in the distance. The Russians were coming! These flashes and explosions continued throughout the night. Then at about 3 am we heard the iron bars moving and the door opened. The guards threw in our pants and boots, telling us we were leaving in 15 minutes. We got out and started marching toward the American lines. We marched till almost noon. We came to a large sand pit. While we were in the sand pit Russian tanks started to fire artillery shells at us. That was all the German guards could take. They left us and ran off in the opposite direction.

"We're free!" We all began shouting for joy at the sight of the Germans running away. The shelling kept up for some time. A couple of the fellas waved a white flag and finally the shelling halted. We chose Andy, from Yonkers, New York, and Ken, from Milwaukee, to go forward and meet the Russians under a white flag and tell them we were Americans. Andy spoke Russian and Ken spoke Polish. We watched as they walked across the field to the Russians. They reached the Russian tank commander. He was a short man with white hair and a neatly trimmed, thick, white mustache. He told Andy and Ken to go back and get us.

We were about a quarter mile from the Russians. As we were running across the field a bunch of American P51 Mustangs came out of nowhere and opened up on us. Not knowing who we were they shot both legs off Big George, and his buddy Little George lost one leg. Both of these guys were from Ohio and they were always together. The Russians took them both to their field hospital. Another casualty crossing the field was Al. Some Russian standing off in some bushes let loose with a round and hit Al in the neck. Lucky for Al nothing vital was hit. Al went off to the hospital with the two Georges. As they were taking Al to the hospital he kept yelling, "Wait for me! Don't leave me!" About an hour later we saw a guy riding a bicycle toward us. It was Al, with his neck all bandaged up. He said the Russians had given him the bike and told not to walk, just to rest.

The Russians started to set up a kitchen right in the middle of the street. They had some very large kettles in which they started to make soup. They were celebrating our freedom right along with us. Of course, to celebrate properly, they brought out some of their supply of vodka. They also had two American trucks, one that was loaded with raw meat, and the other filled with bread, nothing in either truck was wrapped. There were a lot of little German kids running around and the Colonel reached up into the bread truck and took several loaves, tore them apart and threw them to the kids. We knew the kids were hungry by the way they went after those loaves.

The colonel instructed one of his soldiers to bring the vodka from one of the trucks. We had to toast the colonel about a half a dozen times. The colonel could speak pretty good English and he told us to take any of the houses we wanted and not to walk anymore. We ate and drank with the Russian colonel and even offered to help them with their artillery, which we did for several days.

For several restful days we just sat around with the Russians. Sometimes we carried artillery shells for them; but most of the time we just rested and enjoyed our freedom. Then two of our guys, Al and George volunteered to try and make it through the lines to the Americans. They left that night and were gone for several days. About 2 pm, a couple of days later while we drank coffee on the back porch someone shouted, "G.I. trucks!" Here came three 6 x 6's, U. S. Army trucks, down the road guided by Al and George to the house where we were staying. Seeing those trucks was like dying and going to heaven. The driver, a big, black man, named Leo, jumped out and hugged every one of us, "You're going home fellas." We all hugged him right back and just stood there crying for joy. It turned out that the outfit we were taken to was our own 82nd Airborne Headquarters. It was like old home week for five of us–back with the 82nd again. It was the happiest day of our lives!

# FREEDOM & CAMP LUCKY STRIKE

We loaded up on the trucks and, in no time at all, we were rolling. The Russians shouted their goodbyes, calling us the Americanskis. The trip took about two hours and we were back in the midst of the 82$^{nd}$ Airborne Division. I felt I was home after 20 some long months.

I asked around about who was the oldest guy in the outfit, trying to find out who had been there the longest. When they told me I was surprised I had never heard of him. It seems the outfit had been replaced about ten times or more since I was with them.

The first two guys to greet us were the chaplain and the head cook. The chaplain had all kinds of cigarettes and told us when those were gone he would get us more. The cook said they had just finished eating but there was plenty of food left. He brought out a pan of sliced beef. I thought the guys would go nuts. Once again, our emotions were running so high, we all thought we had died and gone to heaven. Everyone ate what they could of the sliced beef. We even had coffee and cake for dessert. Next, they escorted us to a hotel where they put us up for the night. The next morning we got up and had breakfast before heading for the airport at Hildesheim. On the way our trucks passed through the city of Hamburg. Hamburg had been flattened by our bombers. It didn't seem like there was anything in the whole city over three feet high. It was just terrible to see such a large city as this so utterly destroyed–and all for what?

At Hildesheim airport there were a lot of C47s and other transport planes waiting on the tarmac including some fighters, bombers and P51s and P38s at the far end of the airport. We sat around the airfield for a short time and were finally told to load up. We boarded our C47 and one of our fellas saw these boxes full of K-rations which we had never had. In Africa we had only eaten C rations. The crew chief of the plane said to help ourselves, so we all ate K-rations during the trip to France. While in flight we were all given earphones and listened to music. The first song we heard was *Don't Fence Me In.* We all got a kick out of that, thinking it was just for us.

In France we landed at some field, but never did hear it's name. Here we were transferred to a hospital train for the trip to Camp Lucky Strike, near La Harve. We were treated very well on the train which was run by American G.I.s. We were also fed a light meal during the trip.

Camp Lucky Strike was great. We were assigned to tents that housed twelve men. We were all issued a new set of uniforms and we each had our own cot with sheets, blankets and pillows. We were made to feel very comfortable.

Across the road from our tent was the mess hall, used mainly by truck drivers. The head cook was a big man, and one of the nicest guys I'd ever meet. We asked if he would give us something to eat and he'd say, "Sit right down and dig in!" His food was absolutely the best. When the high command found out about our using the mess hall across the street they quickly put a damper on that. They told us and the cook that his food was too rich for us, due to our weakened condition.

At this time I only weighed 113 pounds, down from about 180 before I was captured. I wasn't exactly a heavy weight, and I felt I needed the good food to get my health back. We joked among ourselves that if we stood in the sun and drank tomato juice we would look like thermometers. In fact, we were so thin that we had to stand in the same place twice just to cast a shadow. Our ribs stuck out like suit case handles. Sometimes it seemed like we had to stand on the scale twice to get the needle to move.

The Red Cross set up a tent near us with egg nog and donuts. One of our guys didn't listen to the doctors and with his eyes being bigger than his stomach, he ate several donuts and dropped over dead. The Red Cross immediately closed up shop, no more free donuts for us.

The Army tried to put a little meat back on our bones by feeding us special food in small quantities. They told us our stomachs had shrunk down and so they had food for us all day long. Anytime I got a little hungry I was able to eat a little food at the designated mess hall.

During our stay at Camp Lucky Strike we were checked over from head to foot and given money to go into La Harve. We were also interrogated by the high command. They wanted to know where we were wounded, how many times, what treatment we had for our wounds and what kind of atrocities they put us through. When we were interrogated about the treatment we received from the Germans we all had to sign statements and swear we would never reveal to anyone what took place while we were incarcerated. They were interested in how we had been treated in general by the Germans. The doctors examined all our wounds and treated them the best they could, without admitting us to the hospital. We were also given a new set of clothes: shirt, pants, socks, shoes, cap and Ike jacket. They supplied us with all our insignia: European ribbon, Good Conduct Medal, Parachute Wings, Combat Infantry Badge and Purple Hearts. My Purple Heart came with three oak leaf clusters for being wounded four times: getting my hand and fingers badly cut when I had to grab a German bayonet; when I was hit by shrapnel in the vineyard; getting shot in the butt while trying to crawl on my belly through the vineyard; and the concussion I received when the German officer smashed me in the forehead with the rifle butt.

Now that we all had a little money to spend, we decided to go into La Harve and check out the town. We headed right for the truck driver's tent and asked around if any of them were headed to town. One fella said he would give us a lift. He said whenever we wanted to come back to camp all we had to do was find a truck in town and hitch a lift back.

In Le Havre we just walked around for a couple of

hours, checking out the town. Having worked up a thirst, we headed for one of the town's saloons and ordered some drinks. One of our guys, Clem, could understand and speak a little French. He overheard a group of locals, who were looking us over, talking about us. Clem noted that from their conversation, they hated us. Clem told them off. He told them that if they didn't like us being there, they could leave or we would get rough. Within a couple a minutes they all disappeared. Not one of them were in uniform so we really didn't care. Clem discovered that we were disliked in several different taverns. We let it be known that we really didn't give a darn whether they liked Americans or not. Our attitude was that we Americans freed them of German oppression. They didn't have a response to that.

We went back to sight-seeing and strolling around the town. Seems that most of the people would stare at us. We stopped at a bakery and bought a sack of cookies to munch on. We really had a hard time communicating with these folks. We were even looking to buy some souvenirs, but felt so helpless trying to speak with these people. We had so much trouble communicating we gave up, found a truck and got back to camp in time for supper.

We spent about a month at Camp Lucky Strike while they tried to put some weight on us. Most of our time was spent just lying around doing nothing. As the days passed we began to regain our strength and feel about half normal. Soon we were being told that we would be sailing for home. We said our goodbyes and headed off to the ship, moored in Le Havre's harbor.

# CRUISING HOME

We were loaded on a Liberty Ship, the U.S.S. Sea Porpoise. We knew we were still at war with Japan and wondered about a possible sub out there stalking us, since our ship was sailing alone.

A Liberty Ship is much smaller than the troop ships which had initially brought us to Africa. Most of the passengers on board were ex-POWs. There were also a lot of sergeants on board who were headed for the Pacific where the war was still being engaged. The first day on board I was nosing around and walked into the officer's mess. There was a guy in the kitchen counting dishes and doing inventory. I asked him if he needed help and he said he could use some. Since I had nothing but time on my hands I figured I might as well be busy. He said I could count all the dishes, the cups, knives, forks and spoons. This took about four hours and during this time we became pretty good friends. I don't recall the cook's name now, but he even offered me the opportunity to use the shower in his quarters anytime I wanted. He took me up and showed me his quarters–bedroom, bathroom and sitting room.

Sometime during our afternoon together, a lieutenant, Keene, who was also from St. Paul, came along and asked if I would take charge of the Officers' Mess. I told him I couldn't even boil water, but he told me all I had to do was take charge. He said the other fellas would do all the work. The lieutenant said he already had Ray and Bill, also boys from St. Paul, to take care of the troop mess. So it was all conveniently arranged and I was given a key to the Officers' Mess. I spent my days in the Mess and ate all the corn flakes I could. It seems like a dozen times a day I would have a bowl of corn flakes with condensed milk. At meal time the kitchen help would bring the food down to my kitchen and put it in the steam table. The officers would eat the same food as the troops. The only big difference was that the officers ate off china plates while the troops ate out of their mess kits.

One day the lieutenant came by and told me to wait for him in the kitchen after I locked up for the night. He said he would also send Ray and Bill up to the kitchen after they were finished for the evening. So there we were waiting for the lieutenant. We had no idea why he wanted to see us, and after hours at that. We didn't have to wait long before the lieutenant was pounding on the door, calling for us to open up. He came in with a full case of eggs and a bucket. He set them down and started cracking eggs into the bucket. So we all cracked eggs. Finally the lieutenant took the bucket and, to our surprise, he started making eggnog. For the next couple of hours we sat around the kitchen drinking eggnog. We kept the rest of the eggs and had eggnog feasts for the next couple of nights. This was a real treat for me since I hadn't had anything decent for a long time–the eggnog seemed like a luxury. During one of the eggnog feasts, Ray asked me if I would be his best man at his wedding when he got home. And sure enough, a couple months later, I was the best man at Ray and Marie's wedding.

The cruise home to the United States was much different from the cruise to North Africa. Most notable, we were not in a convoy. It would have been nice to have some other ships around us, because when we were about half way across the ocean our engines quit. For those of you who've never experienced an engine shut down at sea...you don't want to. We bounced around the ocean like a fishing bobber for several hours before the crew got the engines going again.

On both trips we noticed the ocean was full of porpoises. Dozens of them would follow us day and night, waiting for the garbage to be thrown from the stern.

On nice days there would be groups of fellas on the deck shooting craps. Sometimes there would be hundreds of dollars in piles and one time a gust of wind came up and blew most of the money overboard. Someone quickly fell on top of the pile to keep the rest from blowing away.

My time with the Germans didn't dull my sense of humor. One day I walked into the head and there were about twenty guys sitting there, all of them seasick. I couldn't resist, so I asked them, "How many of you fellas would like some greasy pork chops?" In unison they threw up and all shouted at me to get the heck out of there. It was funny, yet it wasn't, to see all of them vomit at the same time. Really a sick bunch.

Every morning one of my duties was to prepare a huge pot of coffee. All I had to do was turn on the steam after I put the coffee grounds in the top. My first customer in the morning was the Catholic Chaplain. He would rap gently on the door and I knew immediately who it was. He would always politely ask if he could have "a cup of that fine coffee you make." I never drank it black because it was so strong it took the enamel off your teeth. I always had to doctor it up to make it fit to drink.

Since I was in charge of the Officers' Mess, after my crew had served the officers and had cleaned up, we all sat down and ate our meals off the fine china too. Then I would often head for the Mess Hall Steward's cabin and just relax in one of his overstuffed chairs. It was easy to see how he rated such opulent quarters with his responsibility for keeping the ship's crew and passengers all fed. The best part of his quarters was the fresh water shower which he permitted me to indulge in every day.

The ship's store was where we would stock up on candy and cigarettes. The store was only open for a limited time each day and there was always what seemed like an endless line. It was like a duty-free store, no taxes at all on any of the merchandise. Cigarettes were the hot item because they were so cheap.

We were still at war with Japan, so we did have to watch for submarines. We were lucky though, and made it across from Europe without incident. The only casualties on our trip were the great number of men who were seasick the whole trip. Seems like a lot of the fellas never left the head–just too darn sick.

As we approached New York harbor we could all see the Statue of Liberty. It seemed like it was way out in the Atlantic. That statue sure looked beautiful to us. As soon as we saw her most of the fellas just stood there and cried–we were so happy to return to the good old United States of America.

Our ship was met outside the harbor by about a dozen boats loaded with cheering people. They were all waving and yelling, happy to see their troops coming home. It was an emotional feeling I will never forget, I could hardly contain myself. We finally landed in New York harbor. As soon as they dropped the gang-plank some of the guys rushed off and got down on their hands and knees and kissed the ground. Everyone had tears of joy! What a happy day for us to touch the U.S.A.

# FURLOUGH

Everybody on the "USS Sea Porpoise" was taken to Camp Kilmer in New Jersey where we spent the night. The next day all the guys from Minnesota were put on a troop train for the Twin Cities. At the various stops along the way, someone would ask the conductor how long we would be in the station. If there was enough time, someone would rush off. Soon they would be seen charging back to the train with a case of ice-cold beer. This went on everytime the train stopped for any length of time. Everyone really wanted to celebrate. Riding on the train was very relaxing. Most of us just sat back and enjoyed the ride. The scenery was just beautiful as we crossed our country.

Finally, after a very enjoyable three day trip, our train pulled into Fort Snelling where we got our orders before going home. My orders stated that I had a 60 day convalescent furlough and then had to report to Hot Springs, Arkansas. Those 60 days went by awfully fast.

My first stop was at my sister Ann's house on Maryland Avenue. At first she did not recognize me. Next I went to my dad's. He was only a couple of blocks away on Marion Street. It was very emotional–dad, Ann and I did a lot of crying. While home, my sister Ann and her husband, Louie, said I could use their car for my running around. She cautioned me though that the tires were pretty bad and that I may be changing one every day. I told her that would be no problem, I would just get some new tires. But Ann explained that tires were being rationed and no one could get tires. I figured, what did I have to lose? I drove down to the local Firestone dealer and asked the manager for a set of tires for the car. He asked me where the heck I had been for the past several years. I told him that I been overseas and had just gotten home. He went over to speak with the mechanic, told him to get the tire size for my car, and to rustle up some new ones for me. I sincerely thanked the man and drove off proudly with a set of new tires. Ann couldn't believe it, she was overjoyed at having new tires. A few days later I decided to buy a 1940 Ford so I could come and go as I pleased.

There was a tavern, Granner's Bar, on Rice Street, that I sort of made my headquarters while I was home. The bar was owned by John who had immigrated from Illmitz, Austria, the home of my mother. John was about 60 years old, single and very generous to me. The bar was a great place to meet a lot of old friends. Well, John approached me one day and proposed making Monday's a special day. He told me to be at the tavern at 8:30 in the morning and several of us would go to his cottage on Forest Lake about 40 miles away. As we left, John always told his bartender Matt that we were going to the lake to cut the grass. We soon found out that John did not even have a lawnmower.

John brought everything we needed–all the food and drinks. After we polished off everything that John brought we would head over to Somerset, Wisconsin where John knew of some bars. It was party time all over again. Finally we would head for home, St. Paul. We sure were careful because none of us could see too well. We were lucky there were not many cars on the road.

The next day, back at Granner's, some of the folks would ask where we had been. We would always tell them,"Up at John's cutting the grass." Those of us who regularly went on these escapades were John, Roy, Cliff, Bob and me. Roy had tried to get into the service. But due to a hunting accident that claimed one of his hands and took the thumb off the other hand, none of the military branches would take him. Cliff was an engineer for the Northern Pacific railroad, and Bob had been medically discharged from the Marines a few weeks after he enlisted.

One fishing trip took us to Brainerd, Minnesota. We were leaving St. Paul around midnight and stopped at Bob's home to gather some gear. While there we noticed his mother

111

had baked a beautiful cake - we left half of it. What a good cake. We got into Brainerd about five in the morning. We were so hungry we decided to have some breakfast before heading to the lake. I was dressed in my uniform and had given all the fellas overseas caps and suntan army shirts. Well, when breakfast was over we were looking for our bill. The waitress told us that the man in the next booth had paid our bill. I got up to thank the man and he told me that anyone shot up like that fellow, pointing at Roy, who had lost his hand and thumb in the hunting accident, is not paying while he was there. We thanked him.

We tried to do something interesting everyday. I was our designated driver because I had no trouble getting gas. Most of my neighbors were leaving me their gas coupons since gas was still being rationed. We found ourselves fishing, or going to baseball games at the Saint's Ball Park on University Avenue. We always got in free because we knew one of their players, Bob, their catcher. But most of my evenings were spent at John Granner's Bar. There were several girls that would come into Granner's looking for me. I was always making some excuse about having to be here or there. Eventually as the night dragged on a big group of us would all sit together and reminisce enjoying our friendship and love of life, while John would keep the drinks flowing.

Another friend was Tin Cup Tschida. When I visited his bar I was always told to sit at a specific booth and Tin would bring a towel with numerous packs of cigarettes. I was told any time I needed more just to come on back.

This new freedom of mine was something special. Only someone who has been a forced laborer for years while incarcerated could possibly understand how I wanted to drink all of life that I could during my short furlough home. I was still anticipating a transfer to the Pacific Theater of war and the invasion of Japan.

One day we planned a visit to our relatives' farm in North Dakota. My brother Rich was home for a few days from the Navy since his ship was in drydock in Portland, Oregon. We packed up the car with Aunt Millie and my sister Ann, and headed west. Our first day we went into Minot with my cousin Dick who had a few errands to run. As I waited for him in my car, a fellow came along and started talking to me about buying my car. He said he would buy it right then and there. I told him it wasn't for sale since I had a long trip ahead of me at the end of the week to get home. Later I mentioned this to Dick and he said that fairly new cars were scarce and hard to come by. Just another reason why I felt so fortunate.

That afternoon, Dick and I headed for the river. When we noticed how many ducks were in the River, we hurried back to the farm for the shotguns. One shot was all it took for each of us to bag a couple of ducks for dinner. My Uncle George was sure glad to have duck that evening.

When it was time to head home, we were overwhelmed with supplies. We took geese for family dinners and Uncle George not only filled our gas tank, but gave us two five-gallon cans for reserves. When we got home we had to wash my brother Rich's seabag which had been in the trunk with the live geese. It was covered with goose crap!

Time was not my friend on this furlough–it was running out fast. After returning from North Dakota, we had a few final get-togethers at Granner's Bar and old John even threw me a surprise send-off party.

# RECUPERATION–ARMY STYLE
# HOT SPRINGS & VANCOUVER

My orders were to report to Barnes General Hospital in Vancouver, Washington by way of Hot Springs, Arkansas. I was to get a complete physical and have all my wounds evaluated. The doctors were going to see what they could do for me. I figured they would patch me up and I would be on my way to the Pacific. An old "top kick sergeant" from northern Minnesota named Phil was also headed back to military life. We had met earlier in France. He said we could take the train together to Hot Springs, Arkansas. Phil and I rode down to Chicago, the first stop on our trip. The train to Hot Springs was not there so Phil and I spent some time wandering around downtown Chicago. Because of this railroad delay we found ourselves to be AWOL. We finally got underway and eventually arrived in Hot Springs.

We were met at the station by a chubby major and two M.P.s. Phil and I were under the impression that these guys were the welcoming committee–boy did we get that wrong! The major told us, in no uncertain terms, that we were AWOL by two days. Phil told him he would have to blame that on the railroad. The major retorted that we were at fault for not allowing enough time for the trip. Well, Phil made some kind of remark to the major, adding that he didn't think the major had seen either ocean, nor had he ever heard a gun fired in anger. And, no, the major did not display a combat infantry badge, as did all of us who served in combat. The major, red-faced by now, reached over and ripped the stripes right off Phil's sleeve. I began to laugh and said, "By golly, Phil, now I out rank you!" The major, not taking kindly to my reaction, reached over and ripped my stripes off! This was a strange situation–here we were, both laughing hysterically and not really caring that we had just been busted.

We got a ride to the hotel from the M.P.s and were

dropped off at the Arlington Hotel. This was a beautiful place. It had everything we needed: hot baths, massage rooms, drug store and restaurant. We signed in and were given very plush rooms. On each floor there was a sergeant, posted at a desk outside the elevator. You simply told him what time you wanted to be called each morning for breakfast. Each of the tables in the restaurant were set for four with bright, white tablecloths. All the waiters were G.I.s, wearing white jackets and pants. All our ordering was done from menus. For the Army this was really high class.

All of us took advantage of the hot baths, followed by relaxing massages. They almost put you to sleep and all you wanted to do when they were through was sleep. It was certainly soothing and restful. Another part of our stay was getting thorough medical checkups: they checked our entire body including our teeth.

While we were in Hot Springs a bunch of us rented a convertible for our two week stay. We drove around town and the surrounding area, often stopping at auctions and open store fronts. The folks seemed to be selling everything imaginable by auction: jewelry and diamonds caught our attention. We found it interesting just to be there listening to the bidding. Often we would just drive out to a nearby lake where we found a beautiful beach for swimming.

During our stay, the Army brought all of our pay up to date. Phil and I both got our stripes back. It was a joy to see Phil with all of his top-kick stripes back on his uniform. Phil was planning to stay in the Army as he already had about fifteen years to his credit. So, Phil and I were soon to be parting company. Phil headed to Georgia for assignment and I was finally headed to Barnes General Hospital in Vancouver, Washington.

There were six of us heading to Washington. I was scheduled for the hospital and the others were going to Vancouver Barracks to earn enough points to get discharged from the service. I had plenty of points to be discharged, and then some; but I had to go to the Army Hospital for further examination.

While en-route to Vancouver we stopped in Kansas City and had a layover of several hours. I wanted to get myself a new pair of shoes. We stopped into a shoe store and I picked out a great looking pair of oxfords. After making my selection the salesman asked if I had an authorization ticket, kind of like a ration coupon. We were dumbfounded, we had no idea what he was talking about, since all we had was cash. He wanted to know where we had been. We told him we'd been out of the country for a while, which the uniforms would have made obvious. The clerk permitted us to pay with cash on our way out.

I was designated as the person responsible for all the other fellas service records. I carried them all in a large envelope that also contained all our meal tickets while enroute on the train. When we went to eat I simply gave the chef a meal ticket for each one of us. We couldn't complain about the trip. We enjoyed such wonderful scenery of mountains and rivers. And to think that some folks pay big bucks to go overseas when they haven't seen half of what this wonderful country has to offer. I believe you appreciate the finer sights of this country more after you have been overseas. Our train traveled for quite some distance along the Columbia River which is just gorgeous.

In Vancouver I left my five traveling partners and headed off to Barnes General. I was the first ex-POW to be admitted there. The staff assigned me to a private room. The chief of staff was a colonel who I got to know pretty well. He would come into the room in the morning and just sit there by the bed and make small talk. On one visit he came in and said he had something for me, it was the Purple Heart medal with my name engraved on the back. When I told him I already had three of them, he said he knew and that I should wear them with pride. I assured him that I would.

During the day the other fellas and I would pass the

time visiting. One day the nurse came in and told me I had visitors. I was shocked, explaining that my home was well over a 1,000 miles away. The nurse said that there were two sailors here to see me and she insisted that one looked kind of like me. To my surprise in walked my brother Rich and one of his buddies. His ship was in dry-dock across the river in Portland and he wanted to show it to me.

The next morning I asked the doctor about leaving to visit the ship. He said it was okay and even provided a car. Bill, the fella in the room across the hall from me, drove. We got to the general vicinity and saw nothing but cyclone fence. When we found a gate and asked where PC787 was, the sailor said, "Right here!" and pointed to where the ship was berthed. He let us in and we started down the pier. About half-way down, we ran into some sailors who asked us who we were looking for. I told them we wanted to see the Chief Gunner and they all yelled for Rich.

Rich showed us around and introduced us to many of his ship-mates. What impressed Bill and I was how small the ship seemed, especially for being out in the middle of the ocean. Rich said that on the way back from the western-Pacific they had run across a typhoon. He said the ship was bobbing around a lot and seemed to have spent more time underwater than on the surface.

The next morning, back at the hospital, it was x-ray time again. It seemed like every morning was x-ray time. I finally asked the colonel when they were going to perform surgery on my back and buttocks to remove the shrapnel and bullets. He surprised me when he said they were still studying the x-rays and that it didn't look like they would be doing any surgery. The doctor was concerned about all the shrapnel between the knuckles of my spine. He said that when they were trying to remove all the pieces, all it would take is one slip and I could be paralyzed. He was pretty certain that all the pieces of metal in my back would stay in place and not move around. As far as the bullets in my rear-end—he said that scar-tissue had developed around them and that they should not prove to be a problem.

All these x-rays were at least providing me and the Army with some answers. My skull had been fractured by the German Captain in the Capua, Italy, train yards and you can still see the outline on my forehead. The colonel was pretty sure that this would not cause me any problem since it seemed to have healed well. Another discovery was that my right leg had grown a little longer than my left since I had broken my legs back at Fort Benning during our third airplane jump. This has never seemed to be a bother and I really don't notice it. The Army finally discharged me on October 6, 1945.

# FINAL NOTE

I still have constant pain in my right foot where it was frost-bitten during our 1,000 mile march in 1945. The bone of the foot is trying to come through the bottom layers of skin and muscle. Without well-designed supporting shoes I can hardly take a step. I've endured two surgeries by the V.A. and yet there could be more done.

I am reminded of the war with every step I take, and some days I stop to reflect . . ..as a result of my years in prison as a German P.O.W., I feel I have learned a lot about human life and the value of it. I have no animosity toward the guards or people who had us incarcerated, as they had a job to do just as we did. And, as the saying goes, "All's fair in love and war." My overall outlook on life is to live every day to the fullest and try to forget the past, because life truly can be wonderful!

All for what? It was all for freedom, my country, my family, my friends and the memory of two German soldiers who shared kindness in the midst of a hell on earth.

# TIMELINE OF EVENTS

June 30, 1942  .  Entered service, Fort Snelling, Minnesota.
April 29, 1943 . . . . . . . . Deported United States for Africa
May 10, 1943  . . . . . . . . Arrived in Casablanca, Morocco
July 9, 1943 . . . . . . . Sicily invasion–Jump near Gela, Sicily
July 13, 1943 . . . . . . . . . . . . . . . . . Captured by Germans
July - August 1943  . . . . . . . . . . . . . . . . . . Capua, Italy
August - October 1943  . . . . . . . . . . . . . . . . Stalag II B
October 1943 - January 1945 . . . . . . . . Schulenberg Camp
January 1945 - February 1945 . . . . . . . . . . . Long March
February 1945 - May 1945  . . . . . . Dettemenn Dorf-Kelso
May 5, 1945  . . . . . . . . . . . . . . Liberated by the Russians
October 6, 1945  . . . . . . . . . . . . . Separated from service

# DECORATIONS

European-African-Middle East Ribbon with two bronze stars
Good Conduct Medal
Purple Heart with three bronze clusters
Presidential Citation
Combat Infantry Badge
Parachutist's Wings
Bronze Star for valor
Ex-Prisoner of War

# GUARANTEED WEIGHT LOSS

## STALAG 2B's
## STANDARD DAILY PRISONER MEAL

### SOUP DU JOUR

1.    Warm up 4 gallons of water

2.    Add one potato

3.    Salt is optional

4.    Once a day have one bowl of the soup with one slice
      of bread.

In memory of Beanie

ISBN 155369807-X